Lecture Notes in Computer Science   13738

More information about this series at https://link.springer.com/bookseries/558

Wang Qingyang · Liang-Jie Zhang (Eds.)

Services Computing – SCC 2022

19th International Conference
Held as Part of the Services Conference Federation, SCF 2022
Honolulu, HI, USA, December 10–14, 2022
Proceedings

Editors
Wang Qingyang 🆔
Louisiana State University
Baton Rouge, LA, USA

Liang-Jie Zhang 🆔
Kingdee International Software
Group Co., Ltd.
Shenzhen, China

ISSN 0302-9743   ISSN 1611-3349 (electronic)
Lecture Notes in Computer Science
ISBN 978-3-031-23514-6   ISBN 978-3-031-23515-3 (eBook)
https://doi.org/10.1007/978-3-031-23515-3

Preface

Services account for a major part of the IT industry today. Companies increasingly like to focus on their core expertise area and use IT services to address all their peripheral needs. Services computing is a new science that aims to study and better understand the foundations of this highly popular industry. It covers the science and technology of leveraging computing and information technology to model, create, operate, and manage business services.

The 2022 International Conference on Services Computing (SCC 2022) contributed to building the pillars of this important science and shaping the future of services computing. The event was a prime international forum for both researchers and industry practitioners to exchange the latest fundamental advances in the state of the art and practice of business modeling, business consulting, solution creation, service delivery, and software architecture design, development, and deployment.

SCC 2022 was one of the events of the Services Conference Federation event (SCF 2022), which had the following 10 collocated service-oriented sister conferences: the International Conference on Web Services (ICWS 2022), the International Conference on Cloud Computing (CLOUD 2022), the International Conference on Services Computing (SCC 2022), the International Conference on Big Data (BigData 2022), the International Conference on AI & Mobile Services (AIMS 2022), the International Conference on Metaverse (METAVERSE 2022), the International Conference on Internet of Things (ICIOT 2022), the International Conference on Cognitive Computing (ICCC 2022), the International Conference on Edge Computing (EDGE 2022), and the International Conference on Blockchain (ICBC 2022).

This volume presents the papers accepted at SCC 2022. We accepted 9 papers. Each was reviewed and selected by at least three independent members of the Program Committee.

We are pleased to thank the authors whose submissions and participation made this conference possible. We also want to express our thanks to the Organizing Committee and Program Committee members, for their dedication in helping to organize the conference and review the submissions. We owe special thanks to the keynote speakers for their impressive talks.

December 2022

Qingyang Wang
Liang-Jie Zhang

Organization

Services Conference Federation (SCF 2022)

General Chairs

Ali Arsanjani   Google, USA
Wu Chou   Essenlix, USA

Coordinating Program Chair

Liang-Jie Zhang   Kingdee International Software Group, China

CFO and International Affairs Chair

Min Luo   Georgia Tech, USA

Operation Committee

Jing Zeng   China Gridcom, China
Yishuang Ning   Tsinghua University, China
Sheng He   Tsinghua University, China

Steering Committee

Calton Pu   Georgia Tech, USA
Liang-Jie Zhang   Kingdee International Software Group, China

SCC 2022

Program Chair

Qingyang Wang   Louisiana State University, Baton Rouge, USA

Program Committee

Sanjay Chaudhary   Ahmedabad University, India
Lizhen Cui   Shandong University, China
Kenneth Fletcher   University of Massachusetts, Boston, USA
Pedro Furtado   University of Coimbra/CISUC, Portugal
Alfredo Goldman   USP, Brazil
Shigeru Hosono   Tokyo University of Technology, Japan

Services Society

The Services Society (S2) is a non-profit professional organization that was created to promote worldwide research and technical collaboration in services innovations among academia and industrial professionals. Its members are volunteers from industry and academia with common interests. S2 is registered in the USA as a "501(c) organization", which means that it is an American tax-exempt nonprofit organization. S2 collaborates with other professional organizations to sponsor or co-sponsor conferences and to promote an effective services curriculum in colleges and universities. S2 initiates and promotes a "Services University" program worldwide to bridge the gap between industrial needs and university instruction.

The Services Society has formed Special Interest Groups (SIGs) to support technology- and domain-specific professional activities:

- Special Interest Group on Web Services (SIG-WS)
- Special Interest Group on Services Computing (SIG-SC)
- Special Interest Group on Services Industry (SIG-SI)
- Special Interest Group on Big Data (SIG-BD)
- Special Interest Group on Cloud Computing (SIG-CLOUD)
- Special Interest Group on Artificial Intelligence (SIG-AI)
- Special Interest Group on Edge Computing (SIG-EC)
- Special Interest Group on Cognitive Computing (SIG-CC)
- Special Interest Group on Blockchain (SIG-BC)
- Special Interest Group on Internet of Things (SIG-IOT)
- Special Interest Group on Metaverse (SIG-Metaverse)

Services Conference Federation (SCF)

As the founding member of SCF, the first International Conference on Web Services (ICWS) was held in June 2003 in Las Vegas, USA. The First International Conference on Web Services - Europe 2003 (ICWS-Europe'03) was held in Germany in October 2003. ICWS-Europe'03 was an extended event of the 2003 International Conference on Web Services (ICWS 2003) in Europe. In 2004 ICWS-Europe changed to the European Conference on Web Services (ECOWS), which was held in Erfurt, Germany.

SCF 2019 was held successfully during June 25–30, 2019 in San Diego, USA. Affected by COVID-19, SCF 2020 was held online successfully during September 18–20, 2020, and SCF 2021 was held virtually during December 10–14, 2021.

Celebrating its 20-year birthday, the 2022 Services Conference Federation (SCF 2022, www.icws.org) was a hybrid conference with a physical onsite in Honolulu, Hawaii, USA, satellite sessions in Shenzhen, Guangdong, China, and also online sessions for those who could not attend onsite. All virtual conference presentations were given via prerecorded videos in December 10–14, 2022 through the BigMarker Video Broadcasting Platform: https://www.bigmarker.com/series/services-conference-federati/series_summit.

Just like SCF 2022, SCF 2023 will most likely be a hybrid conference with physical onsite and virtual sessions online, it will be held in September 2023.

To present a new format and to improve the impact of the conference, we are also planning an Automatic Webinar which will be presented by experts in various fields. All the invited talks will be given via prerecorded videos and will be broadcast in a live-like format recursively by two session channels during the conference period. Each invited talk will be converted into an on-demand webinar right after the conference.

In the past 19 years, the ICWS community has expanded from Web engineering inno-vations to scientific research for the whole services industry. Service delivery platforms have been expanded to mobile platforms, the Internet of Things, cloud computing, and edge computing. The services ecosystem has been enabled gradually, with value added and intelligence embedded through enabling technologies such as Big Data, artificial intelligence, and cognitive computing. In the coming years, all transactions involving multiple parties will be transformed to blockchain.

Based on technology trends and best practices in the field, the Services Confer-ence Federation (SCF) will continue to serve as a forum for all services-related con-ferences. SCF 2022 defined the future of the new ABCDE (AI, Blockchain, Cloud, Big Data & IOT). We are very proud to announce that SCF 2023's 10 colocated theme topic conferences will all center around "services", while each will focus on exploring different themes (Web-based services, cloud-based services, Big Data-based services, services innovation lifecycles, AI-driven ubiquitous services, blockchain-driven trust service ecosystems, Metaverse services and applications, and emerging service-oriented technologies).

The 10 colocated SCF 2023 conferences will be sponsored by the Services Society, the world-leading not-for-profit organization dedicated to serving more than 30,000 services computing researchers and practitioners worldwide. A bigger platform means bigger opportunities for all volunteers, authors, and participants. Meanwhile, Springer will provide sponsorship for Best Paper Awards. All 10 conference proceedings of SCF 2023 will be published by Springer, and to date the SCF proceedings have been indexed in the ISI Conference Proceedings Citation Index (included in the Web of Science), the Engineering Index EI (Compendex and Inspec databases), DBLP, Google Scholar, IO-Port, MathSciNet, Scopus, and ZbMath.

SCF 2023 will continue to leverage the invented Conference Blockchain Model (CBM) to innovate the organizing practices for all 10 conferences. Senior researchers in the field are welcome to submit proposals to serve as CBM ambassadors for individual conferences.

SCF 2023 Events

The 2023 edition of the Services Conference Federation (SCF) will include 10 service-oriented conferences: ICWS, CLOUD, SCC, BigData Congress, AIMS, METAVERSE, ICIOT, EDGE, ICCC and ICBC.

The 2023 International Conference on Web Services (ICWS 2023, http://icws.org/2023) will be the flagship theme-topic conference for Web-centric services, enabling technologies and applications.

The 2023 International Conference on Cloud Computing (CLOUD 2023, http://thecloudcomputing.org/2023) will be the flagship theme-topic conference for resource sharing, utility-like usage models, IaaS, PaaS, and SaaS.

The 2023 International Conference on Big Data (BigData 2023, http://bigdatacongress.org/2023) will be the theme-topic conference for data sourcing, data processing, data analysis, data-driven decision-making, and data-centric applications.

The 2023 International Conference on Services Computing (SCC 2023, http://thescc.org/2023) will be the flagship theme-topic conference for leveraging the latest computing technologies to design, develop, deploy, operate, manage, modernize, and redesign business services.

The 2023 International Conference on AI & Mobile Services (AIMS 2023, http://ai1000.org/2023) will be a theme-topic conference for artificial intelligence, neural networks, machine learning, training data sets, AI scenarios, AI delivery channels, and AI supporting infrastructures, as well as mobile Internet services. AIMS will bring AI to mobile devices and other channels.

The 2023 International Conference on Metaverse (Metaverse 2023, http://www.metaverse1000.org/2023) will focus on innovations of the services industry, including financial services, education services, transportation services, energy services, government services, manufacturing services, consulting services, and other industry services.

The 2023 International Conference on Cognitive Computing (ICCC 2023, http://thecognitivecomputing.org/2023) will focus on leveraging the latest computing technologies to simulate, model, implement, and realize cognitive sensing and brain operating systems.

The 2023 International Conference on Internet of Things (ICIOT 2023, http://iciot.org/2023) will focus on the science, technology, and applications of IOT device innovations as well as IOT services in various solution scenarios.

The 2023 International Conference on Edge Computing (EDGE 2023, http://the edgecomputing.org/2023) will be a theme-topic conference for leveraging the latest computing technologies to enable localized device connections, edge gateways, edge applications, edge-cloud interactions, edge-user experiences, and edge business models.

The 2023 International Conference on Blockchain (ICBC 2023, http://blockc hain1000.org/2023) will concentrate on all aspects of blockchain, including digital currencies, distributed application development, industry-specific blockchains, public blockchains, community blockchains, private blockchains, blockchain-based services, and enabling technologies.

Contents

The Data Visualization Analysis in Global Supply Chain Resilience Research During 2012–2022

Lijun Li[1,2] , Rui Chi[3], and Yusou Liu[3]

[1] Guizhou University of Commerce, Guiyang, China
[2] School of Management, Universiti Sains Malaysia, Penang, Malaysia
[3] The TIANFU College of SWUFE, Mianyang, China
liuyushou@tfswufe.edu.cn

Abstract. Supply Chain Resilience (SCR), which is the capacity to return the supply chain to its starting condition, which is necessary when the system is compromised by hazards (externally), is one of the most critical supply chain management concerns in the worldwide post-COVID-19 era. This article aims to examine influential journals, publication types, research headings, scholars, and citation metrics in the SCR field, to assist researchers globally in better understanding the knowledge map of the subject and identifying frontiers. The findings indicate that SCR is an important and widespread issue in the post-COVID-19 era, with 2,278 articles published on the Web of Science over the study period. Tableau Public was used in data analytics during the research period. The finding of this research is that (1) the majority of publications were published in SCIE and/or SSCI. (2) The journal-published papers were easier than book, conference, and series publications. (3) Future researchers will be able to conduct more in-depth research on the Multi-topics of SCR, such as people, COVID-19, the food supply chain, and the service industry. (4) Numerous researchers have already participated in SCR-related research, establishing a solid academic community research foundation. This is a review of SCR research and research ideas to complete a future study on the resilience of China's agricultural product supply chain.

Keywords: Bibliometric · Data analytics · Supply chain resilience (SCR) · Tableau public · Visual analysis · Web of science

1 Introduction

The outburst of COVID-19 was a severe challenge, as the closures and production suspensions due to the pandemic and the physical distancing were faced by the supply chain global. To minimize supply chain interruptions caused by the pandemic, maintaining a regular supply chain is one of the most significant global supply chain management concerns in the post-COVID-19 era. Different studies have highlighted that a potentially viable solution that can be used to avoid the risk of supply chain disruption is improving supply chain resilience (SCR) (Ali, 2021; Christopher, 2004; Dubey, 2017; Jain, 2017).

W. Qingyang and L.-J. Zhang (Eds.): SCC 2022, LNCS 13738, pp. 1–11, 2022.
https://doi.org/10.1007/978-3-031-23515-3_1

SCR is a prominent transdisciplinary idea in supply chain research while relatively young. Holling (1973) created the notion of resilience, and other researchers extended this concept into the management field and proposed the concept of SCR, which is typically translated as: supply chain resilience and supply chain elasticity in Chinese. Sun (2017) describes SCR as the capacity to return the supply chain to its starting condition, which is necessary when the system is compromised by hazards (externally).

In this study, Tableau Public was used to undertake bibliometrics and visualization analysis using technologies of cluster analysis (publication types, journal, authors, keywords). Through the compilation of 2278 document records from the Web of Science (WoS) into a scientific atlas, the organization and evolution of SCR research from 2012 to 2022 were meticulously mapped out. This article aims to examine influential journals, keywords, scholars, and publications in the SCR field, to assist researchers globally in better understanding the knowledge map of the subject and identifying frontiers. The remainder of this work is structured as follows. In Sect. 2, bibliometrics and data sources are introduced. In Sect. 3, the results of the bibliometrics are presented. In Sect. 4, the main subjects and effective knowledge systems are discussed. Section 5 summarizes the research.

2   Methods and Sources of Data

2.1   Methods

This study focused on the Scientometric analysis, a technology from the field of knowledge that demonstrates the knowledge's structural relationships and development process. Data visualization is a process of visualizing data and information collected by big data, with charts, maps, and graphs. CiteSpace, Looker, Tableau, and Zoho Analytics are the acclaimed visualization technology of researchers. Tableau, a product of a computer science project from Stanford, was developed in 2003 and was one of the most widely used software for bibliometric data analysis. The objective of Tableau is to assist users in viewing and comprehending data (Anonymous, 2022). With Tableau, Alex (2022) explores in visualization the prevalence of alcoholic drinks and cigarette products among young people in India. The visual analysis by Tableau Public, based on the data and information of SCR, can analyze the current state and future of SCR.

2.2   Data Sources

The keyword 'SCR' were utilized throughout the research process. The topic 'SCR' was used to search the WoS database for English-language published articles between 2012 and 2022 and 2279 results were found, as illustrated in Table 1 and Fig. 1. Between 2012 and 2021, the number of papers published kept growing. In 2021, 30 times as many papers will be published as in 2012. Affected by the COVID-19 outbreak, related research has surged, with 1,377 June 2020–2022 papers comprising 60% of the total (2278). As of June, 332 papers have been published in 2022, which is about half the amount of papers released in 2021. Anticipating that the number of publications published in 2022 would climb further.

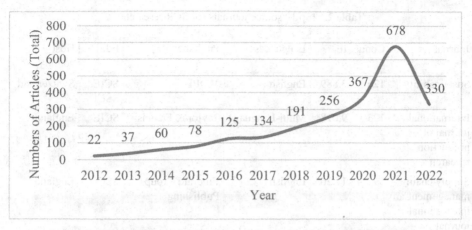

Fig. 1. Total Number of WoS Indexed Articles between 2012 and 2022

Table 1. Data retrieval program

Retrieval mode	Publication type	Document type	Year	Retrieval results	Retrieval time
Supply Chain Resilience	Article, conference, book, series, patent	An article, early access, review article, meeting, or other	2012–2022	2278	25th June 2022

3 Results of Scientometric

Through visual analysis, the objective of this work is to examine and record significant points and development pathways of SCR from 2012 to 2022. Based on WoS, the first part visually analyses the journals of SCR research. The second part analyses the publication types of SCR research. The third part analyses the authors of SCR research. The fourth part analyses the citation metric of SCR research.

3.1 Visual Analyses of Journals

This section discussed the publication of works in various periodicals. As shown in Table 2, 603 papers were published in the top 10 source journals. More than 25 percent of the total number of SCR papers were published in the WoS between 2012 and 2022. Sustainability (126), International Journal of Production Research (123), and Supply Chain Management-an International Journal (59) include the most published papers (Philsoophian, 2021). The only journal excluded from SCIE and/or SSCI is the Benchmarking an International Journal, including ESCI.

    Table 2 lists the top ten SCR research journals, including influential variables. Sixty percent of the top 10 journals originated from England, twenty percent from the Netherlands, one from the United States, and one from Switzerland. Following the publisher's

Table 2. Top 10 source journals for SCR research

Journal	Count	IF	Languages	Publisher	Edition	Host country
Sustainability	126	3.889	English	MDPI	SCIE, SSCI	Switzerland
International journal of production research	123	9.018	Multi-Language	Taylor & Francis	SCIE	England
Supply chain management-an international journal	59	11.263	English	Emerald Group Publishing	SSCI	England
International journal of logistics management	54	5.446	English	Emerald Group Publishing	SSCI	England
Journal of cleaner production	54	11.072	English	Elsevier SCI	SCIE	USA
International journal of production economics	51	11.251	English	Elsevier	SCIE	Netherlands
Annals of operations research	39	4.820	English	Springer	SCIE	Netherlands
International journal of operations & production management	36	9.360	English	Emerald Group Publishing	SSCI	England
Computers & industrial engineering	33	7.180	Multi-Language	Pergamon-Elsevier Science	SCIE	England
Benchmarking an international journal	28	--	English	Emerald Group Publishing	ESCI	England

Note IF = Impact factor in 2021.

visual studies, an intriguing phenomenon was uncovered. Four journals are published by Emerald Publishing, one of the world's foremost digital-first publishers. The other six journals are published by Elsevier, Elsevier SCI, MDPI, Pergamon-Elsevier Science,

Springer, and Taylor & Francis, among others. Utilize the top ten source journals in the linguistics-related visual study. All of the top 10 journals accept papers in English. Also, two of the 10 journals accept additional languages.

3.2 Visual Analyses of Publication Types

Figure 2 shows the publication types of 2278 papers. The visual analysis shows that all papers on SCR research publish in four publication types (book, conference, journal, and series). The majority of SCR papers (96%) are published in a journal, followed by conferences (1.8%), series (1.4%), and books (2%). Consequently, SCR researchers globally are more likely to publish research results in a scientific journal.

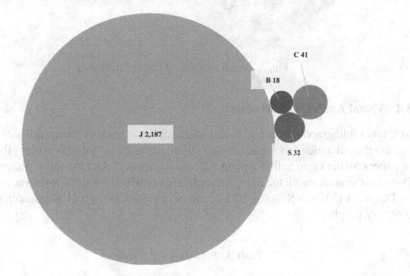

Fig. 2. Publication types

3.3 Visual Analyses of Research Headings

Figure 3 displays the top 10 research headings from 2287 papers examined visually. Headings centered first on Humans (74), followed by COVID-19 (29) and food supply (27), and then Animals (25) and pandemics (fourth and fifth, respectively) (19). Therefore, future study trends will concentrate on SCR pertaining to humans, COVID-19, food supply, etc.

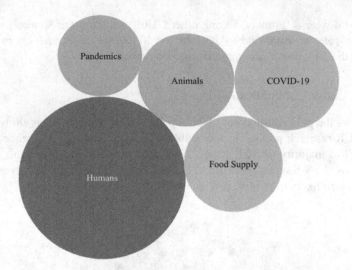

Fig. 3. Visual analyses of research headings

3.4 Visual Analyses of Scholars

In 2278 bibliographic records, visual studies of the authors were utilized. Figure 4 depicts the outcome of the visual analysis with part authors. Table 3 displays the number of papers by the same author among 2278 total papers. Select the top 3 authors. Ivanov D (68) is the author with the most extraordinary contributions to SCR research, followed by Dolgui A (33) and Sokolov B (27), and both collaborate on SCR research regularly, typically jointly.

Table 3. Published Top 5 authors

S/N	Author	Count
1	Ivanov D	68
2	Dolgui A	33
3	Sokolov B	27
4	Rajesh R	21
5	Paul S K	17

3.5 Visual Analyses of Citation Metric

Table 4 mentioned the 20 most-cited articles according to the WoS citation measure. Following a visual study of the citation measure, the article authored by the top two authors in the top publish is also the most cited. Ivanov D's publications have been cited more than 2100 times. Dolgui A ranked second and has also approached 1,000 times.

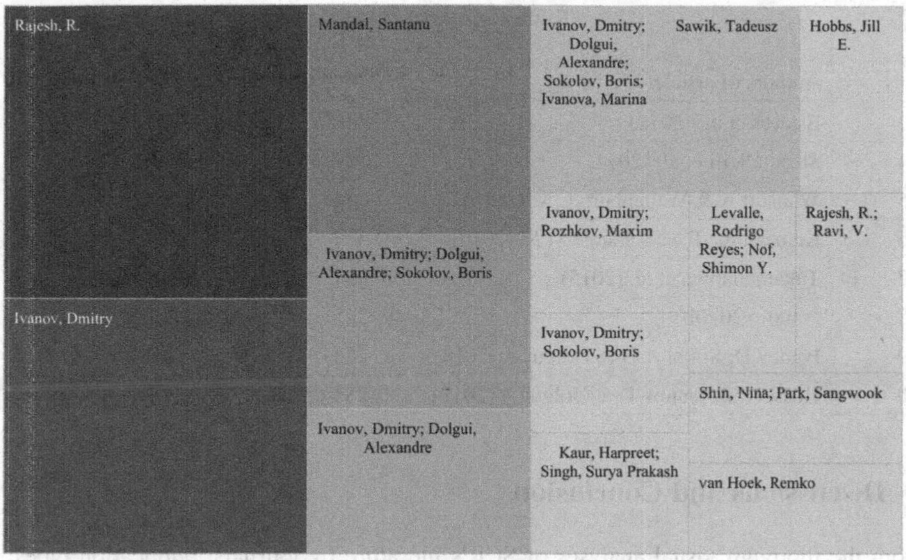

Fig. 4. Visual analyses of part authors

The number of citations of Hosseini S's works has reached 987, the same as those of Dolgui A, despite simply did not make the list of the top five authors in the top published.

Table 4. Top 20 articles of citation in WoS

S/N	Authors of article	Total cittions	Publish year
1	Hosseini et al. (2016)	704	2016
2	Ahi et al. (2013)	661	2013
3	Ivanov (2020a)	478	2020
4	Aven (2016)	449	2016
5	Heckmann et al. (2015)	433	2015
6	Ivanov D & Dolgui A (2020)	421	2020
7	Ivanov D, Dolgui A & Sokolov B (2019)	419	2019
8	Oro et al. (2013)	404	2013
9	Brandon-Jones et al. (2014)	379	2014
10	Hobbs (2020)	367	2020
11	Ambulkar et al. (2015)	353	2015
12	Petti et al. (2013)	346	2013

(continued)

Table 4. (*continued*)

S/N	Authors of article	Total cittions	Publish year
13	Esteves et al. (2012)	340	2012
14	SteadteSeifi et al. (2014)	337	2014
15	Wieland A & Wallenburg C M (2013)	331	2013
16	Kamalahmadi M & Parast M M (2016)	327	2016
17	Tukamuhabwa et al. (2015)	287	2015
18	Ivanov (2020b)	285	2020
19	Ivanov D, Sokolov B & Dolgui A (2014)	285	2014
20	Hosseini S, Ivanov D & Dolgui A (2019)	281	2019

4   Discussions and Conclusion

From the thorough visual analyses of SCR's literature by journals, publication types, research headings, scholars, and citation metrics, in the worldwide post-COVID-19 era, both the industry (agriculture, food processing, and other industrial products, etc.) and the service industry will face the risk of supply chain disruption (Afrasiabi, 2022; Chung, 2022; Dasgupta, 2022; Diem, 2022; den Nijs, 2022; Hobbs, 2021; Niyigena, 2022; Plana, 2021; Qazi, 2022; Tan, 2022; Weitzel, 2021; Zhang, 2021). Therefore, SCR Research is necessary to ensure the efficient operation of the global supply chain. Although this systematic review is based on a small sample of journal articles, the findings suggest that:

Following the visual analyses of Journals, most publications were published in SCIE and/or SSCI. Sustainability, International Journal of Production Research, and Supply Chain Management-an International Journal were among the top publications in the number of articles published (Philsoophian, 2021). These publications include important research that can be used to develop ideas.

Concerning publication types, everything was claimed that journal-published papers were easier than book, conference, and series publications. This means that journals can deliver superior study results to researchers. Moreover, journals might give a better venue for the presentation of results by researchers.

Examining the available research headings of SCR reveals that the current study focuses mainly on humans, COVID-19, and the food supply chain. In the future, academics can do more in-depth research in these areas, particularly research on SCR worldwide in the post-COVID-19 period. In addition, it is therefore advised that related research be expanded to include service industry SCR research.

Examining the analyses of scholars and citation metrics reveals that, in addition to the research of five researchers, namely Ivanov D, Dolgui A, Sokolov B, Rajesh R, and Paul S K, several scholars have conducted a productive study on SCR. Based on these existing studies, future related research may be conducted. These studies, the academic community has generally acknowledged, can also serve as a foundation for future innovation (Ivanov, 2020a; Ivanov, 2020b; Ivanov et al., 2014, 2019, 2020).

Acknowledgments. This study was funded by Mianyang Social Science Key Research Base - 2022 Project of Sichuan Modern Circulation Economy Research Center, Tianfu College, Southwestern University of Finance and Economics (XDLTJJ2022YB02).

References

An extended hybrid fuzzy multi-criteria decision model for sustainable and resilient supplier selection. *Environ. Sci. Pollut. Res.* **29**(25), 37291–37314

Ahi, P., Searcy, C.: A comparative literature analysis of definitions for the green and sustainable supply chain management. J. Clean. Prod. **52**, 329–341 (2013)

Ali, M.H., Suleiman, N., Khalid, N., Tan, K.H., Tseng, M.L., Kumar, M.: Supply chain resilience reactive strategies for food SMEs in coping to COVID-19 crisis. Trends Food Sci. Technol. **109**, 94–102 (2021)

Alex, S., Satheesh, N., Vanitha, K., Shenbagavalli, P.: Data analytics and visualisation using tableau on prevalence of alcoholic drinks and tobacco products among young people in India. In: Innovations in Computer Science and Engineering, 2022, pp. 245–261 (2022)

Ambulkar, S., Blackhurst, J., Grawe, S.: Firm's resilience to supply chain disruptions: Scale development and empirical examination. J. Oper. Manag. **33**, 111–122 (2015)

Anonymous. *What Is Tableau? | Tableau* (2022), 6–25. https://www.tableau.com/why-tableau/what-is-tableau

Aven, T.: Risk assessment and risk management: review of recent advances on their foundation. Eur. J. Oper. Res. **253**(1), 1–13 (2016)

Brandon-Jones, E., Squire, B., Autry, C.W., et al.: A contingent resource-based perspective of supply chain resilience and robustness. J. Supply Chain Manag. **50**(3), 55–73 (2014)

Christopher, M., Peck, H.: Building the resilient supply chain. Int. J. Logist. Manag. **15**(2), 1–13 (2004)

Chung H. Variable work schedules, unit-level turnover, and performance before and during the COVID-19 pandemic. *Journal of Applied Psychology* (2022)

Dasgupta, S., Robinson, E.J.Z.: Impact of COVID-19 on food insecurity using multiple waves of high frequency household surveys. Sci. Rep. **12**(1), 1–15 (2022)

den Nijs, K., Edivaldo, J., Châtel, B.D.L., et al.: A global sharing mechanism of resources: modeling a crucial step in the fight against pandemics. Int. J. Environ. Res. Public Health **19**(10), 5930 (2022)

Diem, C., Borsos, A., Reisch, T., et al.: Quantifying firm-level economic systemic risk from nation-wide supply networks. Sci. Rep. **12**(1), 1–13 (2022)

Dubey, R., Gunasekaran, A., Childe, S.J., Papadopoulos, T., Blome, C., Luo, Z.: Antecedents of resilient supply chains - an empirical study. IEEE Trans. Eng. Manage. **66**(1), 8–19 (2017)

Esteves, A.M., Franks, D., Vanclay, F.: Social impact assessment: the state of the art. Impact Assess. Proj. Appraisal **30**(1), 34–42 (2012)

Heckmann, I., Comes, T., Nickel, S.: A critical review on supply chain risk–definition, measure and modeling. Omega **52**, 119–132 (2015)

Hobbs, J.E.: Food supply chains during the COVID-19 pandemic. Can. J. Agric. Econ. Rev. Can. Agroecon. **68**(2), 171–176 (2020)

Hobbs, J.E.: The COVID-19 pandemic and meat supply chains. Meat Sci. **181**, 108459 (2021)

Holling, C.S.: Resilience and stability of ecological systems. Annu. Rev. Ecol. Syst. **1973**(4), 1–23 (1973)

Hosseini, S., Barker, K., Ramirez-Marquez, J.E.: A review of definitions and measures of system resilience. Reliab. Eng. Syst. Saf. **145**, 47–61 (2016)

Hosseini, S., Ivanov, D., Dolgui, A.: Review of quantitative methods for supply chain resilience analysis. Transp. Res. Part E: Logistics Transp. Rev. **125**, 285–307 (2019)

Ivanov, D.: Predicting the impacts of epidemic outbreaks on global supply chains: a simulation-based analysis on the coronavirus outbreak (COVID-19/SARS-CoV-2) case. Transp. Res. Part E: Logistics Transp. Rev. **136**, 101922 (2020)

Ivanov, D.: Viable supply chain model: integrating agility, resilience and sustainability perspectives—lessons from and thinking beyond the COVID-19 pandemic. *Ann. Oper. Res.* 1–21 (2020)

Ivanov, D., Dolgui, A.: Viability of intertwined supply networks: extending the supply chain resilience angles towards survivability. A position paper motivated by COVID-19 outbreak. Int. J. Prod. Res. **58**(10), 2904–2915 (2020)

Ivanov, D., Dolgui, A., Sokolov, B.: The impact of digital technology and Industry 4.0 on the ripple effect and supply chain risk analytics. Int. J. Prod. Res. **57**(3), 829–846 (2019)

Ivanov, D., Sokolov, B., Dolgui, A.: The Ripple effect in supply chains: trade-off 'efficiency-flexibility-resilience' in disruption management. Int. J. Prod. Res. **52**(7), 2154–2172 (2014)

Jain, V., Kumar, S., Soni, U., Chandra, C.: Supply chain resilience - model development and empirical analysis. Int. J. Prod. Res. **55**(22), 6779–6800 (2017)

Kalafsky, R.V., Conner, N.: Exploring the dynamics of globalization: Supply chain vulnerability to natural disasters. J. Geogr. High. Educ. **39**(1), 173–181 (2015)

Kamalahmadi, M., Parast, M.M.: A review of the literature on the principles of enterprise and supply chain resilience: major findings and directions for future research. Int. J. Prod. Econ. **171**, 116–133 (2016)

Niyigena, A., Girukubonye, I., Barnhart, D.A., et al.: Rwanda's community health workers at the front line: a mixed-method study on perceived needs and challenges for community-based healthcare delivery during COVID-19 pandemic. BMJ Open **12**(4), e055119 (2022)

Qazi, A., Simsekler, M.C.E., Gaudenzi, B.: Prioritizing multidimensional interdependent factors influencing COVID-19 Risk. Risk Anal. **42**(1), 143–161 (2022)

Oro, D., Genovart, M., Tavecchia, G., et al.: Ecological and evolutionary implications of food subsidies from humans. Ecol. Lett. **16**(12), 1501–1514 (2013)

Pettit, T.J., Croxton, K.L., Fiksel, J.: Ensuring supply chain resilience: development and implementation of an assessment tool. J. Bus. Logist. **34**(1), 46–76 (2013)

Philsoophian, M., Akhavan, P., Abbasi, M.: Strategic alliance for resilience in supply chain: A bibliometric analysis. Sustainability **13**(22), 12715 (2021)

Plana, D., Tian, E., Cramer, A.K., et al.: Assessing the filtration efficiency and regulatory status of N95s and nontraditional filtering face-piece respirators available during the COVID-19 pandemic. BMC Infect. Dis. **21**(1), 1–13 (2021)

Sarkar, S., Kumar, S.: A behavioral experiment on inventory management with supply chain disruption. Int. J. Prod. Econ. **169**, 169–178 (2015)

SteadieSeifi, M., Dellaert, N.P., Nuijten, W., et al.: Multimodal freight transportation planning: a literature review. Eur. J. Oper. Res. **233**(1), 1–15 (2014)

Sun, J.W., Sun, X.Y.: Research progress of regional economic resilience and its application in China. Econ. Geogr. **2017**(10), 1–9 (2017)

Tan, L., Wu, X., Guo, J., et al.: Assessing the impacts of COVID-19 on the industrial sectors and economy of China. Risk Anal. **42**(1), 21–39 (2022)

Tieman, M.: Halal risk management: combining robustness and resilience. *J. Islamic Mark.* 2017 (2017)

Tukamuhabwa, B.R., Stevenson, M., Busby, J., et al.: Supply chain resilience: definition, review and theoretical foundations for further study. Int. J. Prod. Res. **53**(18), 5592–5623 (2015)

Weitzel, J., et al.: Understanding quality paradigm shifts in the evolving pharmaceutical landscape: perspectives from the USP quality advisory group. AAPS J. **23**(6), 1–8 (2021). https://doi.org/10.1208/s12248-021-00634-5

Wieland, A., Wallenburg, C.M.: The influence of relational competencies on supply chain resilience: a relational view. Int. J. Phys. Distrib. Logistics Manage. **43**, 300–320 (2013)

Zhang, J., Qi, L.: Crisis preparedness of healthcare manufacturing firms during the COVID-19 outbreak: digitalization and servitization. Int. J. Environ. Res. Public Health **18**(10), 5456 (2021)

Can an Artificial Intelligence System Be Taken as a Legal Subject

Jianming Shen(✉) (iD)

Hankou University, Wuhan, China
whshen2010@163.com

Abstract. The rapid development of artificial intelligence is increasingly becoming an important factor affecting social life and the legal system. The development of artificial intelligence has taken different category, among which the one with the greatest impact on law and society is the general artificial intelligence represented by NARS, which has sufficient self-learning ability and is exploitable and adaptable to the external world. Such AI agents have the potential to be taken as legal subjects, impacting the framework of the existing legal system. Human subjectivity is legally embodied as legal personality and rights capacity. The most fundamental meaning of legal personality and capacity is indeed the subjectivity of human beings established in modern times, which is rooted in the rational ability of "man to legislate for nature". NARS, for example, realizes this rational ability to "legislate for nature" in a conceptual sense by means of non-axiomatic logic. Such an artificial intelligence should have the possibility to be taken as a legal subject.

Keywords: Artificial intelligence · Legal personality · Capacity for rights

1 Overview and Category of Artificial Intelligence

"Artificial intelligence" was born in an academic conference in 1956 at Dartmouth in the US. Several outstanding young scientists gathered to discuss the issues of intelligence, who did their research on mathematics, neuroscience, computer science, psychology and many other aspects. The concept of Artificial Intelligence was proposed by John McCarthy in the conference. The main goal of artificial intelligence is attempted to achieve human intelligence on computers and research results have emerged in endlessly from the beginning. Every achievement of artificial intelligence has different features and functions. For example, Siri focuses on speech recognition, AlphaGo focuses on machine learning, expert systems focus on inference with domain knowledge, and so on. The results of AI have different characteristics and functions, and can be broadly classified into three categories in terms of the relationship between the external behavior of AI and innate design and learning.

The first type of AI whose outwardly manifested behavior is only related to its innate design and is not capable of acquired learning. The skills or functions possessed by this type of AI are unique, and no amount of later design can change its innate functions.

There are many AI products in this category, such as smartphones, computers, cars, etc. The characteristic of this class of AI is that its ability behavior is only influenced by the innate design, and the acquired learning and training are meaningless.

The second type of artificial intelligence is not only related to innate design, but also this type of AI is capable of machine learning. This type of AI is initially set to have certain functional characteristics and has some prototype of machine intelligence, and only after a later learning and training process does it slowly master this skill or perform certain operations or behaviors. For example, AlphaGo was designed by Google to have the initial skills of Go, and it was only after a lot of data training or machine learning that AlphaGo was really able to master the skills of Go. AlphaGo is a good illustration of this type of AI, which initially has a clear function, and through machine learning and other means, its functional characteristics tend to be perfected and eventually reach a stable state, thus completing machine learning. The functions or behaviors of this class of AI are subject to both limitations from initial design and influences from later learning. In this class of AI, the initial design plays a crucial role in determining that the AI actually has a certain skill, as well as in determining the possibility and significance of later learning training.

The third category of AI is that which also has a predetermined design of an intelligent system that is also capable of learning, but this learning is not limited to a particular domain and can be broad and non-domain specific. The predetermined design of such an intelligent system is only a framework for thinking; it is the training and learning that are more fundamental factors in shaping this type of AI. The first thing that distinguishes this type of AI system from the second type of AI system is that the innate design of the system does not have a clear and specific functional orientation; such systems are only responsible for thinking, reasoning, computing, decision-making, etc., and are open to the tasks and needs of the external world. Specific functions and operations need to be determined according to the problems and goals in practice, and are also adaptive to the external world, so this type of AI does not have a particular single or closed function, and shapes its capabilities based on learning and experience. The typical representative of this type of AI is the NARS system designed by Prof. Pei Wang of Temple University, and also some artificial general intelligence systems. The most important feature of NARS is adaptability, that is, NARS is able to respond to future situations with limited knowledge and relatively insufficient resources, and respond to unlimited needs with limited resources.

The relationship of the function and characteristics of these three types of artificial intelligence between design and learning can be shown in the figure (Fig. 1) .

Because the acquired learning training is related to the time factor, the longer the time, the more adequate the machine learning will be. Therefore, the functions and capabilities of AI can be represented in the following graphical way. The first type of AI is also the one whose capabilities depend only on pre-design, so it is represented as a straight line, such as a smartphone, which has only those functions. The second type of AI is influenced by both innate design and acquired learning, but their functional capabilities are closed and through training will also converge to a certain state of perfection in the end, so the second type of AI presents as a curve with a gradual slope towards 0, such as AlphaGo. The third type of AI is developed for the external world because it has only

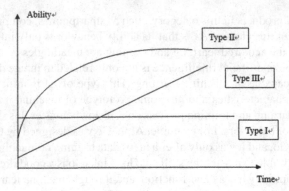

Fig. 1. Category of artificial intelligence

one learning frame of mind innately, and the acquired learning makes it possible to have different functions and capabilities. Thus, as learning continues to strengthen over time, the capabilities of the third AI are also being strengthened. Thus, it appears roughly as a straight line with a constant slope. These three categories are also categorized to be called as the first one is no intelligence, the second one is professional AI, and the third one is AGI, or artificial general intelligence (AGI), and it can be seen from the image that intelligence is actually their slope. AGI because its goal is to achieve human intelligence, and the level of human intelligence is an invariant, so the intelligence of AGI is also presented as a straight line. There is no possibility of a curve with an increasing slope, and that would be what the media call super AI.

2   The Influence of Artificial Intelligence on the Law

These three types of AI agents have had or are having a profound impact on our society, and the impact of the first two types of AI has been much discussed and researched. However, the three types of AI that have the most profound impact on our society and legal system have been relatively little studied. This paper focuses on the impact of the third type of AI, i.e., general-purpose AI.

Under the current legal framework, there are only two possible types of legal regulation of artificial intelligence in legal relationships: one is as an object, the object of direct reference to the rights of human subjects; the other is as a subject, regulated by law. Artificial intelligence, especially the third category of artificial intelligence, can be self-learning, capable of reasoning and decision-making, how to carry out the regulation of the law becomes a difficult problem. The current artificial intelligence is approaching the goal of "how to achieve human intelligence on computers" from one aspect or the whole aspect. Especially under the condition of accelerated development of technology, it is not impossible to realize human intelligence and recreate a kind of intelligence. The ultimate goal of artificial intelligence is to create "intelligent people". Therefore, for this kind of artificial intelligence agents with general intelligence, how to regulate them by law, how possibly becomes the fundamental challenge of artificial intelligence for the law. This is reflected in the legal problem of whether AI can be taken as a subject of law.

This question is the most central issue of AI research. Whether AI should be taken as a legal subject becomes a prerequisite for the regulation of AI by law. The different qualifications of legal subjects, the means and ways of regulation of artificial intelligence by law also have a large difference, while all the rights and obligations of artificial intelligence are also different. This problem is also the core issue that legal practitioners should think about. And the research of artificial intelligence in a certain sense is in the creation of new social activities of the subject, these activities may have a part of human intelligence and ability, but also may have the general human intelligence and ability, and nowadays artificial intelligence also tends to have all the human intelligence this direction, that is, whether the general artificial intelligence can be recognized as "human". Therefore, the legal characterization of artificial intelligence agents should also become an important topic of legal research

And this challenge has reflected in whether the artificial intelligence agents can be taken as a legal subject. This problem might to be the most central legal issue in artificial intelligence research. A prerequisite for the regulation of artificial intelligence by law is to decide whether artificial intelligence should have the qualifications of the legal subject and become the prerequisite for the regulation of artificial intelligence by law. Different legal qualifications have different methods to regulate the artificial intelligence, and different rights and obligations will be possessed. Artificial intelligence research is essentially to create a new "person". The "person" may have a part of the human knowledge and ability, may also have the general human knowledge and ability. Today artificial intelligence is also developed to be equipped with the general intelligence of human. So, can the artificial general intelligence agent be considered to a "person"? It's a vital topic for legal scholar to research legal entity qualitative problem of artificial intelligence.

3 Artificial Intelligence and Legal Subject

The discussion of the law on the qualification of subjects has always been an unavoidable subject in all branches of law and jurisprudence. The provisions on the subject of law are mainly concentrated in the civil law and even the constitution of each country. Civil law is called "the mother of all laws", and many legal principles and values are derived from civil law, and the provisions of civil law on subjects, legal personality and legal capacity have become the basis of all sectoral laws.

3.1 Relative Description of Legal Subject

The main subjects of law stipulated in the General Principles of Civil Law of China include: naturally born person, legal persons, and unincorporated organizations. The establishment requirements of each subject are stipulated. Naturally born person is equipped with civil rights capabilities since he was born and lasts till his death, he can exercise his legal rights and undertake his obligations. As a living organism, a naturally born person has the capacity of rights, which is the basic element to become a legal subject.

Legal person are organizations that are equipped with capabilities of rights and ability to act independently according to law which are established legally and have their own names, institutions, locations, properties and fund. Rules about the third type of legal subject in civil law are assemble to legal person in some aspects and the difference is clearly regulations about the third type is that whether qualification of a manager is needed when organization is established. The function of a manager like the department which makes policy for legal person. In this way, both these two types of organizations need to initiate an institution to make policies, perform and legally represent them to qualify legal subject. Naturally born person is the same when it comes to expressing wills. This means that only when a person or organization can clearly express themselves can they be qualified legal subject, then rights and obligations.

The criterion to judge whether a person could be legal subject in law is capacity of rights, which he is entitled to exercise rights and do corresponding obligations. Capacity of rights is a kind of qualification or ability which means legal subject is allowed to do something and forbidden to do something according to law, it can be regarded as legal personality. German Civil Code started with the chapter of personality and the first rule is that given birth means the beginning of capacity of rights. In this way, legal personality equals to capacity of rights. What is legal personality? In the System of Contemporary Roman Law by Savigny, personality is responsible person in legal relationship, and the essence of it is capability to establish a certain connection in relationship. Legal relationship is exactly the connection between personalities.

However, from the perspective of the History of Law, the concept of legal personality and capacity of rights cannot be the same. Let's take an example of personality in Roman Law. Personality doesn't equal to capacity of rights in Roman Law, it is the identity that support the whole system of Roman Law. A person could only be allowed to do something when he was in certain status, like father's rights toward children and wife in family. Not every organism or naturally born person had full legal personality, besides, if someone had violated the law, the consequence might be the decrease of personality. Therefore, a person had to qualify the identity standard by law to possess legal personality. Professor Junju Ma thinks that the distinctions of term Personality is consequence of different status between different identities. The result of distinctions in law is the separation of organism between legal person. Personality in Roman Law clearly described its essence. Furthermore, the separation of a person and personality means there will be issue of determining whether a person is qualified to have personality in law. It means as follow: what kind of organism is qualified to be a person with legal personality and under what circumstance. The term personality as well as legal technique objectively reflects ancient Roman's view of world and value. Consequently, as the essence of personality, identity legally depart a person and identity on the one hand, on the other hand, it makes personality a legal term with content of ethical value.

With the history of Western world in middle age and the Renaissance, human began to understand and realize the knowledge of themselves. Status of human had improved, and the content of personality include ration and moral values. Therefore, Karl Larenz thought that every person is equipped with capability of rights because everyone in essence is a person with full personality in ethic world. General ration and ethic require the law to admit that every person have capability of rights no matter what. Savigny hold the same opinion, he argued that since all the law was the moral and ethical being which meant that law was just the opinion for every person of the world in their inner free mind, so the original concept of legal subject or personality should be same as concept of human. Personality is more general without identity and become symbol of free will and ration. Comparing with capacity of rights, personality is more abstract which can describe legal status and qualification of subject more generally. Thence, Hegel said that personality included capacity of rights. And personality was so abstract that it was the foundation and being of essence and formality of law.

Therefore, concept of personality and capacity of rights in legal term is not exactly the same. Personality is more of ethical and moral meaning while capacity of rights is more of legal technique and less ethic. After the extract and abstraction by law, personality lost original content and only remain its elements in formality. The word Capacity of Rights was created in German Civil Code, it's both used for naturally born person and legal person (corporation, company, etc.). Community is included in legal subject, there is no doubt that capability of rights is empirical law term. In this way, the standard to determine whether a person is legal subject is to examine whether that object qualifies capability of rights. Capability of rights, as the consequence of development of law lately, is a purely legal technique term in empirical law, it also leaves room for expanding scope of legal subject. Under this circumstance, community can be legal subject with capability of rights and the scale of subject with capability of rights will increase with abundance of social life.

3.2 The Philosophical Connotation of Legal Subject

The substantive content of legal personality would be supposed to be recovered in German classical philosophy, which has nourished the German Civil Code. In this respect, Kant's philosophy provides sufficient nutrition for our current legal theory. It is the main content of Kant's philosophy to think about "what is man". And this content also enriches the connotation of legal personality. It will be better to respond to our legal status of artificial intelligence when we understand the form and substance of legal personality.

Kant argues that reason is the ability of our mind to be able to integrate empirical material into knowledge. Any knowledge consists of two parts: form and material. All knowledge begins with experience, but not originate from it. Empirical knowledge gain from our innate sensations, intuitions, perceptual consciousness. But the content which we gain is accidental. But the form or the frame structure is innate. Therefore, knowledge is integrated form the sensible material, which come from acquired experience, through the intellectual initiative to regulate and integrate. Moreover, Objective things constitute a cognitive object only through the active role of the subject. Without the participation of the subject, objective things cannot be said to be objects of knowledge. All knowledge begins with experience. Once begun, in turn, we have to reflect and analysis on such accepted knowledge, and know what it is or not. Therefore, Kant said, "Thinking without intuition is empty; intuition without concept is blind". In the process of cognition formation, a man does not simply passively accept emotional material outsides, but active in combining the external sensible materials with the innate form of the subject itself. Through "transformation", "provisions", "comprehensive", "integration" actively, knowledge can be gained. In the course of object conforming to concept, human become the legislators of nature. So that, the ability to gain knowledge is that we have the ability to specify the perceptual material through our a priori intellectuality. Kant incorporates the unity of cognition and general necessity into the subjective initiative of self-consciousness, and exclude interference from God beyond our cognitive ability. It's really the first time to establish a person the dominant position in the nature in theory.

Thus, what is core of subject is the ability to legislate in this way, and this ability to legislate lies in the reason of the self and the ability of the self to unify sensual phenomena. The process of man legislating nature is also the process of forming knowledge by using reason. As a rational subject, man should have this legislative ability. This ability is expressed in two aspects, the innate ability of knowing and the acquired experience of perception. Knowing is unity, a kind of self-consciousness, which can unify and integrate all the materials of experience, and is a kind of subject's ability. The subject is able to unify and integrate the acquired perceptual material through logic and other means, to know, and to acquire knowledge. Thus, in the field of cognition, man is the legislator of the natural world and knows the world objectively in conformity with the subjective through the unifying activity of knowing reason.

The ideas of classical German philosophy, represented by Kant, were digested and absorbed by the German legislation. The doctrine of the subject of Kant's philosophy provided the theoretical basis for the determination of the legal subject, personality and capacity of rights in Germany. The free will of man becomes the ethical basis of personality, and it is due to the property of free will of personality that personality becomes the source of all laws. In the social state, reason sets down those principles which are in accordance with distributive justice and those rights which are acquired on the basis of long-term use and are guaranteed by positive law. Among other things, the spirit of subject matter is the spiritual foundation of the entire German civil law, and this spirit of subject matter is embedded in the free will and rational spirit of man and personality. Personality is also a bearer in legal relations, and free will and reason become presupposed conditions in legal relations. The formalized law also mechanicalizes those concepts that have ethically significant content, and in this sense, personhood and capacity for rights are equated. And the right capacity, as the formal meaning of personality, becomes the subject of rights and obligations, and loses the original ethical meaning of personality. Personality also becomes not only the basis of civil law, but also connected with the basic law and the constitution, and becomes synonymous with freedom and dignity, and personality takes on a sacred character.

3.3 Artificial Intelligence and Legal Personality

One can be called a "legal person" because he has capability of rights, and the substance of capability of rights derives from his personality. Personality is the ability of a rational and free willed subject to regulate and legislate. In other words, in law world, in the vision of law, personality is the ability to establish, change, eliminate legal relationship. But what kind of artificial intelligence can be capable of this? According to Kant's theory, it provides us with a beautiful blueprint for artificial intelligence. Kant divides the process of human cognition into two parts, that is, an integrated analysis of sensible experience and rational faculty. This rational faculty to unify perceptual experience, the most significant way of which is what Kant calls a priori logic. Logic is regarded as regular pattern and approach to learn knowledge and the most important methods to realize intelligent in the aspect of artificial intelligence. The conclusion that can be made without any exaggeration is that Kant's philosophy has made full preparation for artificial intelligence at this point.

As for artificial intelligence, this kind of system might include two parts. One is the input of external sensory material. The other is the analysis of the input of the inductive material. That is perceptual ability section and intellectual ability section. According to Kant 's theory, the intellectual ability section could be able to reflect the ability of artificial intelligence as legal personality. Its main task is to organize these input materials into a coherent, meaningful world experience. And intellectual ability is to find out the law of human cognition. And Kant think, logic is the law of thinking, so he created the transcendental logic. And the study of logic is further in-depth. And the logic applied for the artificial intelligence might be different from our human. Because it's essentially different between man and artificial intelligence. But the rules of thinking might be common, and the artificial intelligence is designed to imitate our mind. So, in that case, the Kantian theory provides great blueprint and fine cognitive model. Our cognitive process generally contains two elements. One is low-level cognition, which is information processing from different senses. The second is high-level cognition, which is that the subject, through the access of concept and idea, understand the situation in the conceptual level, extract the meaning from situational experience. With object recognized into the abstract formal framework, situation would be understood as a whole.

In addition, there is huge difference between legal person and naturally born person. The subject of legal is a hypothesis based on rational people. A rational person is formalized through the law, excluded from personality, preferences, emotions and other irrational factors. Because the legal positivism made the study of law more professional and become a strict subject. Such rational person is more adaptable for artificial intelligence. Therefore, from this level, more artificial intelligence can be given the status of the legal subject.

In this case, it is important to note that the legal subject of artificial intelligence is philosophical abstract status. That is, artificial intelligence has the possibility of becoming a legal subject. This legal subject status is also abstract, is the possibility of becoming a legal subject. Artificial intelligence agents to meet the conditions discussed above, it is possible to become the subject of the law and as for what kind of subject, it's required in the specific legislation to be clearly defined. In other words, it's prerequisites and prerequisites for artificial intelligence becoming legal subject to have the rational ability for natural legislation and the ability to regulate self-control. And this abstract legal subject on the one hand is reflected the influence on our current legal system, and out daily life, on the other hand is a response of law on intelligent agent with similar capabilities. Therefore, the artificial intelligence agent can become the legal subject is abstract, only to express the possibility of artificial intelligence agents have become the subject of law. This subject may be a fake "person", a legal person possibly, or another subject possibly. Similar to the "electronic people" in EU legislation, the specific legal status of artificial intelligence needs to be responded and clarified in specific legislation.

4 Non-axiomatic Reasoning System and Legal Personality

Non-Axiomatic Reasoning System, short from NARS, is designed and created by Pei Wang, a professor of Temple University. NARS is a computer reasoning system for achieving general intelligence. And NARS can learn from interaction and experience. And faced with unspecified situation and questions, it can do operations and answer different questions.

4.1 NARS and Its Basic Reasoning Rules

The design of NARS is based on the belief that the essence of intelligence is the capability to adapt to the environment and to work with insufficient knowledge and resources. NARS uses a new form of term logic, or an extended syllogism, in which several types of uncertainties can be represented and processed, and in which deduction, induction, abduction, and revision are carried out in a unified format. The Assumption of Insufficient Knowledge and Resources has become the logical premise of the NARS, and under this assumption and design, NARS has the following characteristics.

Finite: the system's computing power, as well as its working and storage space, is limited;

Real-time: the tasks that the system has to process, including the assimilation of new knowledge and the making of decisions, can emerge at any time, and all have deadlines attached with them;

Open: no restriction is imposed on the relationship between old knowledge and new knowledge, as long as they are representable in the system's interface language.

Adaptable: the system can accommodate itself to new knowledge, and adjust its memory structure and mechanism to improve its time and space efficiency, under the assumption that future situations will be similar to past situations.

These characteristics are the basic features of the NARS and are different from the current mainstream artificial intelligence. In order to achieve the goal of artificial general intelligence, to achieve rational, NARS reasoning system has the following components:

A formal language for the communication between the system and the environment;

An interpretation of the formal language that makes its sentences correspond (maybe loosely) to human knowledge represented in natural language;

An inference engine with some inference rules to carry out tasks, such as match questions with knowledge, generate conclusions from promises, and derive subquestions from questions;

A memory that stores the tasks to be processed, and the knowledge according to which the tasks are processed; and

A control mechanism that is responsible for the choosing of premise(s) and inference rule(s) in each step of inference, and the maintaining of the memory.

NARS is composed of these basic parts, the core of which lies in the first three parts. The first three parts constitute the basic reasoning system of NARS. NARS reasoning system is to rely on the logic, which is to study the rules of thinking, and apply the method of logic to achieve intelligence. NARS logic is different from our daily formal logic, is a non-axiomatic logic (NAL). NARS has nine logical reasoning system configurations; each level has its own syntax and inference rules. And the reason why the whole system is not axiomatic, is that the designer of the system, don't fix the knowledge base of the entire system, and don't give the knowledge base a proposition in the form of axioms, after preset after each level of reasoning rules of system. And all the knowledge of NARS can also be improved and enriched constantly based on the experience and interaction of system. NARS also constantly interact with the outside world in its open structure and obtain new knowledge and awareness under the guidance of the initial reasoning rules.

The NARS has modified and expanded the traditional classical logic, using a new set of non-axiomatic logic under the assumption that knowledge and resources are relatively insufficient. NARS development takes a gradual approach, at each stage, the logic is expanded, giving the system a more expressive language, richer semantics and greater reasoning rules. In general, NARS has the four stages of NAL, including basic reasoning, first-order reasoning, high-level reasoning and procedural reasoning. Among them, the most characteristic of NARS is the way of identifying things. That is, the truth-value function of NARS. For a given statement, if the amounts of positive and total evidence are written as $w+$ and w, respectively, then the truth-value of the statement is represented as a pair of real numbers in $[0, 1]$, $<$ frequency, confidence $>$, where frequency $= w+ / w$, and confidence $= w/(w + k)$. (k is a constant, it means that NARS compares its current evidence to the future evidence. For example, if $k = 1$, NARS always compares this evidence to the next time.) This is not only the way of expression, but also a judgement of object and things. The judgement will be a kind of knowledge. Thus, NARS interprets a judgment in w instances, where the positive instances have $w+$, and the confidence is $w/(w + k)$, and NARS believes the statement at the extent of $w/(w + k)$.

Consequently, truth-value in NARS uniformly represents several types of uncertainty, including randomness, fuzziness, and ignorance. Defined in this way, Non-Axiomatic Logic has an experience-grounded semantics where the meaning of each term and the truth-value of each statement are determined according to the relevant experience of the system, by the system itself. So, the way of cognition of NARS is similar with our human.

The truth-value function of NARS is common in structure of cognition and judge-ment. This innate structure of cognition is relevant to logic, but the content of cognition and knowledge is connective with experience. Only in the participation of the material of experience, a judgement with content can be constituted. NARS contains other reasoning rules in addition to the basic reasoning rule of the truth-value function.

The basic reasoning is mainly through the truth function to form knowledge and judgment. First-order reasoning is to extend the non-axiomatic logic in the way of adding the knowledge and judgment obtained in the previous stage into the rules of language and grammar; through the way of set theory to define the relationship between different judgments. High-level reasoning is to allow statements to be used as terms, through deduction, induction, abduction, syllogism or other aspects of the way to high-level reasoning. In addition to the above three levels of logical reasoning process, another special feature of NARS is procedural reasoning, the fourth stage of reasoning. In this stage, time has been introduced. Procedural reasoning means to infer about events, operations, and goals. At this stage, an event is defined as a special type of statement that with temporal truth-value, that is, its truth-value can change over time. Operations are the means for the system to achieve goals. NARS can carry out some external operations and internal control. The execution of an operation is usually accomplished by a mechanism outside the reasoning system, such as a hardware device with certain sensor/effecter capability, or another computer program with certain information-processing capability. The reasoning system interacts with them by issuing execution commands and collecting execution consequences, and these activities consist of the sensorimotor processes of the system as a whole. Operations toward the outside of the system correspond to perception and control of the environment. Operations toward the inside of the system correspond to self-perception and self-control. Therefore, NARS is not only to absorb new knowledge and answer new questions, but also to achieve a variety of operations, in the process of interaction with the external. Under the original goals and independent goals, NARS can uniformly handle goals/operations and ordinary tasks/beliefs by modifying the internal architecture and control mechanisms, and ultimately can become a relatively independent artificial intelligence reasoning system.

4.2 NARS and Legal Personality

Artificial Intelligence system is totally different from a person in essence. Human is natural creature with many special biological features. Our brain also evolves to adapt the change of nature. But artificial intelligence system does not develop as human does, it is the simulation of human's brain which in essence is a digital system without any biological features. Artificial intelligence system like NARS do have something in common with human. Can NARS be a legal subject?

The key of status of being legal subject is rational capability and freedom to legislate for the nature and human being themselves. Human as subject is foundation and origination of all regulations, which means that subject is capable to set regulations and orders, and this kind of capability is absolutely initiative and beyond themselves to legislate. This capability is basic content of personality, and it is the necessary element of qualifications to be legal subject.

The mode of cognition of NARS is based on a set of truth-value function which NARS can understand and make judgment with available knowledge. Truth value of NARS is defined with F (frequency) and C (confidence), and both these two values are gradually formed and modified in the process of interacting with externals. Therefore, NARS is directly related to experiences.External experiences are input into NARS and the mode to deal with data is NAL. These reasoning rules have many levels and ranks to deal with different data separately. There is basic logic to understand and judge the certain subject, and elementary reasoning rules to handle the relationship between subjects, and high order rules for different sentences and different variables.Reasoning rules which related to logic and set theory and math in themselves are predesigned in NARS and gradually become the method for NARS to know the external world. In this way, truth-value function of NARS is composite of innate logical reasoning rules and acquired experiences. The content of subject and knowledge comes from experience in the design of innate logical rules. This kind of cognitive mode happen to be same as Kant's intellectuality. With cognition and integration by NARS, knowledge about materials from externally objective experience can be shaped and modified finally. Therefore, NARS is capable of cognitively understanding this world and own knowledge at this point.

Besides, NARS system is capable of regulate itself and achieve its goal. In NARS's reasoning process, the system itself can make procedural reason, make judgment of events and operations and goals, which means that the system does not only learning to observe, it also operates. a goal is defined as a statement to be made true (or as close to true as possible) by executing operations. In this way, a goal can be represented as an event, whose preconditions and postconditions can be gradually revealed through reasoning on available knowledge, and eventually related to operations. For certain operation, the system can describe the preconditions (causes) and postconditions (consequences) of a given operation, and carry out explaining, predicting, planning, and skill learning by reasoning on these descriptions.The original goal of NARS system can probably come from maker's design, or can be entitled by its users or managers which is pretty random for the system. But once original goal is given and set, designer cannot have control over other derived goals by system itself. The realization of every goal need integration and qualification of many elements, NARS system can illustrate the condition and process of realization of goals by reasoning rules. All available conditions and elements can be new goals of NARS system. With these reasoning process carrying on, original goals are not important anymore because new goals can independently be system's goal. In this kind of process, NARS system can absolutely control itself. In the meantime, when the goal of NARS system was defined, all its operations require acquired learning. The system can only know procedures to operate through experiences. After many times of operations, NARS has to acquire skills to operate, and more importantly, it has thoughts and can reflect itself. In this way, NARS system will gradually know that it is different from external world and then it will realize independence itself by reflection. The sense of self for NARS will finally shape in this process. The reasoning system exerts control by issuing orders and collecting results of former orders. Operations for external world correspond to knowledge and control of environment, and operations for internal system correspond to self-cognition and self-control.

The former several levels of reasoning rules make preparations for procedural reasoning and form knowledge base for system itself. The system establishes and carries out goals and plans in this knowledge base by decision-making procedure and realize its own goals. In this process, reasoning system keeps collecting and issuing orders and achieves self-control and management. The operation is the reflection by system itself and NARS also needs this kind of reflecting-operation to avoid making mistakes and even assess afterwards. It is the reflection that makes NARS realizes its existence by itself. Furthermore, reasoning system also controls external devices' operations to contribute to realization of goals. This means that the system can sense and control external condition, and in the process of goals' realization and expectations, knowledge and control about system itself become deeper. It makes the sense of self and self-regulation of system more prominent through dividing the insides form the outsides and the subject from the object. So that, the system has achieved the self, but also regulated the self, also have the ability to create, change and eliminate a specific social relationship or legal relationship.

In result, NARS has such ability of awareness and execution, which is the essential connotation of legal personality. Especially, legal personality is abstracted and formalized. Through legal positivism, and gets rid of ethics and morals gradually. It's necessary condition for NARS to becomes a true legal subject. Therefore, NARS can be given the qualifications of the corresponding legal subjects, with the capacity of rights.

5 Conclusion

Law and jurisprudence must respond in a timely manner to the profound impact of artificial intelligence on society, particularly general artificial intelligence, and the many implications and risks that go hand in hand with such challenges. And with many social sciences mired in division and controversy, only law can respond institutionally on behalf of humanity. Among the many tasks that need to be accomplished, one of the first steps in the legal regulation of AI is the legal positioning of AI. Whether artificial intelligence can be taken as a legal subject, whether it enjoys the subject qualification of assuming rights and performing obligations. The legal subject or the capacity of rights is closely related to the rational capacity of human beings, so it becomes necessary to explore the conditions and the possibility of the qualification of AI to be taken as the subject of rights from the level of legal philosophy in the abstract. With the rapid development of technology and the in-depth research of artificial intelligence, there will be more and more such artificial intelligence with rational ability, and artificial intelligence will gradually become an important part of our society. The law should also take more comprehensive consideration of the characteristics and capabilities of AI in order to better play the role of law. In the future, in an era of human-machine coexistence, the law will not only be a law for people, but also a norm for other intelligences.

References

1. Schmidhuber, J., Thórisson, K.R., Looks, M. (eds.): AGI 2011. LNCS (LNAI), vol. 6830. Springer, Heidelberg (2011). https://doi.org/10.1007/978-3-642-22887-2
2. Chalmers, D.J., French, R.M., Hofstadter, D.R.: High-level perception, representation, and analogy: a critique of artificial intelligence methodology. J. Exp. Theor. Artif. Intel. 4, 185–211 (1991)
3. Deng, X.: Lectures on German classical philosophy. Hunan Education Press, Changsha (2010)
4. Friedrich Carl von Savigny: The System of Contemporary Roman Law, translated by Zhu Hu. China Legal Publishing House, Beijing (2010)
5. Kant, I.: The Collection of Three Critics, translated by Xiaomang, D., Zutao, Y. Renmin Press, Beijing (2009)
6. McCarthy, J.: What is artificial intelligence? (2004). https://www-formal.stanford.edu/jmc/index.html
7. Karl, L.: General Theory of German Civil Law, translated by Wang X., Shao J. Law Press (2003)
8. Li, Y.: The rational person and its foundation in civil law, legal research (2005)
9. Kurzweil, R.: The singularity is near: when humans transcend biology, translated by Dong, Z., Li, Q. Mechanical Industry Press, South Norwalk (2011)
10. Boden, M.A.: The Philosophy of Artificial Intelligence, translated by Liu, X., Wang H. Shanghai Century Press Group, Shanghai (2006)
11. Ma, J.: The formation, development and vicissitude of the technology of distinguishing the person in nature and the person in law: concurrently on capacity for rights in the civil code of Germany, Modern Law Science (2006)

12. Mo, H.: Private law expansion of subject philosophy: a study of right capability, Law Press (2012)
13. Nilson, N.J.: Artificial intelligence, translated by Zheng, K., Zhuang, Y. Mechanical Industry Press, South Norwalk (2003)
14. Wang, P.: What Do You Mean by "AI"? 2008. https://cis.temple.edu/~wangp/
15. Wang, P.: From NARS to a thinking machine (2007). https://cis.temple.edu/~wangp/
16. Wang, P., Goertzel, B.: Introduction: aspects of artificial general intelligence (2006). https://cis.temple.edu/~wangp/
17. Wang, P.: Toward a unified artificial intelligence (2004). https://cis.temple.edu/~wangp/
18. Russell, S.J., Norvig, P.: Artificial intelligence: a modern approach, translated by Yin J., Zhu E., etc. Tsinghua Press, Beijing (2013)
19. Xu, Y.: Mind language and machine: the dialogue of Wittgenstein's philosophy and artificial intelligence science, Renmin Press, Beijing (2013)
20. Xu, Y.: The prototypes of the very idea of artificial intelligence in the 17th and 18th century European philosophy. Fudan Journal (Social Sciences) (2011)
21. Yang, Z., Deng, X.: The essence of kant three critics, Renmin Press, Beijing (2001)

Context Preserving Data Augmentation for Sequential Recommendation

Benjamin Amankwata and Kenneth K. Fletcher[✉][iD]

University of Massachusetts Boston, Boston, MA 02125, USA
{benjamin.amankwata001,kenneth.fletcher}@umb.edu

Abstract. Item representation learning is a fundamental task in Sequential Recommendation (SR). Effective representations are crucial for SR because they enable recommender systems to learn relevant relationships between items. SR researchers rely on User Historical Interactions (UHI) for effective item representations. While it is well understood that UHI inherently suffers from data sparsity, which weakens item relation signals, seldom considered is the fact the interaction between users and items is mediated by an underlying candidate generation process susceptible to bias, noise and error. These limitations further distort the item relationships and limit the learning of superior item representations. In this work, we seek to amplify weak item relation signals in UHI by augmenting each input sequence with a set of permutations that preserve both the local and global context. We employ a multi-layer bi-directional transformer encoder to learn superior contextualized item representations from the augmented data. Extensive experiments on benchmark datasets for next-item recommendations demonstrate that our proposed SR model can recover item relational dynamics distorted during the candidate generation process. In addition, our approach leads to learning superior item representations for many next-item state-of-the-art models employing RNNs and self-attention networks.

Keywords: Context · Sequential recommendation · Recommender systems · Transformers · Data augmentation

1 Introduction

It is firmly established that the temporal ordering of items is important for next-item recommendation. The ordering of items has been shown to encode relationships between item pairs, contextual information and evolving user preferences [33]. Techniques using Recurrent Neural Networks (RNNs) have been shown to be very effective in next-item recommendation precisely for their ability to encode sequences in discrete time steps that naturally captures the ordering of individual items [6,7,13]. More recently, RNNs have been overshadowed by transformers [31] that employ an attention module that computes similarity scores for all pairs of positions in an input sequence. This in theory, allows transformers to better encode positional dynamics than RNNs where the information

W. Qingyang and L.-J. Zhang (Eds.): SCC 2022, LNCS 13738, pp. 26–40, 2022.
https://doi.org/10.1007/978-3-031-23515-3_3

encoded between pairs of positions in a sequence degrade the further apart those positions are.

Despite the generally acknowledged significance of item order in the input sequence, little work has been done to investigate the impact of item order augmentation on the next-item recommendation problem. The recent foray of contrastive learning (CL), a self-supervised representation learning approach originating in computer vision (CV) into SR, is bringing focus to the significance of item order for representation learning in SR [16,35]. The benefits of data augmentation to self-supervised representation learning are well studied in CV [4,28] and have accompanied CL in its application to SR. The handful of available works employing CL for SR has also adapted data augmentation techniques from CV that indirectly interrogate the impact of item order in SR.

Unlike in natural language processing (NLP), where syntax naturally imposes a rigid structure on the order and position of tokens, user historical interactions (UHI) is induced over a set of items by a candidate generation process e.g., a retrieval system, or a recommendation engine. This process is susceptible to bias, noise, and error. We argue that rigidly adopting the item ordering of the candidate generation process is sub-optimal to item representation learning because the stated limitations distort the fundamental relationship signals between items. Any downstream tasks that utilize these item representations will thus suffer performance degradation due to this distortion.

In this work, we propose a two-stage approach to mitigate biases and distortion in UHI stemming from the underlying candidate generation process called **COM**binatorial **BERT** (COMBERT). Our work builds on long standing work on distributional hypothesis [23] and more recent work on interactional context for SR [1]. In the first stage, we amplify item co-occurrence and interactional context signals with a permutation-based data augmentation approach that is constrained by preserving local (sub-sequence level) and global (full sequence level) interactional context. We adapt strongly restricted permutations (SRP) to accomplish both objectives. In the second stage we employ a self-supervised pre-training approach that leverages the amplified contextual and item relation signals to learn superior contextualized item representations. The output of the second stage is a 3-D representation of UHI[1] which is fed to a 2-D CNN for next-item prediction. Experiments show that our representation learning approach produces superior item embeddings not just for our proposed SR model but also for the majority of compared next-item models employing RNNs and self-attention. We summarize the main contributions of this work as follows:

- we propose an effective self-supervised approach for recovering and amplifying item relation signals for superior item representation learning.
- we propose an efficient algorithm to create and sample diverse UHI sequences for data augmentation that preserves both local and global contextual information.

---

[1] The 3-D representation of UHI is created by concatenating 2-D representation of all the items in the UHI in their original order.

– we propose an approach for next-item recommendation that significantly outperforms the majority of state-of-the-art (SOTA) baselines on seven public
datasets.

2   Related Work

2.1   Sequential Recommendation (SR)

Early works on SR adopted Markov Chains to learn item transition patterns
in UHI [9,22]. With the advent of deep learning (DL), RNNs became favored
for SR [11]. More recently convolutional neural networks (CNNs) and graph
neural networks (GNNs) have also been successfully applied to SR [27,34]. A
major development in the DL approaches to SR was the introduction of neural
attention mechanisms [2] to enable selective emphasis on different items in user
historical interactions (UHI) when modeling sequential patterns. Inspired by the
success of self-attention networks in NLP [31] a number of transformer-based
SR models have been proposed [12,26] which employ transformer layers to learn
item transition patterns in UHI.

2.2   Data Augmentation

Very recently, a handful of works have begun to explore data augmentation
techniques for SR with promising results. Xie et al. [35] propose three data augmentation strategies for SR. The first, *Item Crop*, randomly selects and deletes
a continuous subsequence of UHI. The second, *Item Mask*, randomly drops a
proportion of items from UHI and the third, *Item Reorder*, randomly shuffles
a continuous subsequence of items. Liu et al. [16] extend the above approach
by leveraging item correlations to generate augmented sequences. They propose
Substitute where a set of indices in UHI are selected at random and the items
at those indices are respectively replaced with correlated items. Wu et al. [32]
propose augmentation methods for sequences represented as graphs. Similar to
Item Drop, *Node Dropout* discards a fraction of nodes together with their connected edges. *Edge Dropout* is analogous but only discards edges. *Random Walk*
combines *Node Dropout* and *Edge Dropout* to generate subgraphs for each input
sequence representation.

2.3   BERT Embeddings

Learning effective item representations is arguably the most fundamental task
in SR. Major recent advances in SR can be directly attributed to advancements
in item representation learning techniques developed in NLP. Distributed vector representation models developed by early neural language models such as
Word2Vec [19] and GLOVE [21] were adapted to learn item representations in SR
[8,30]. In the last few years, neural language modeling has been dominated by the
transformer [31] equipped with a self-attention module that computes similarity

scores for all pairs of positions in an input sequence. BERT [5], a transformer based language model, has peaked the interest of SR researchers because of its ability to encode sentence-level properties within single-word embeddings [18]. This enables the learning of item representations that retain properties about the structure of the input sequence, sometimes referred to as contextual item embeddings. Traditionally, downstream tasks of the BERT model take the output of the final transformer layer as the default representation. However, recent works have uncovered rich contextual information in all layers of the transformer and spurred new research into harnessing and leveraging this information. It has also been shown that different layers of the transformer encode different types of information that may be relevant to different downstream tasks. Song et al. [24] use an LSTM network to connect all intermediate representations of the CLS token The output of the last LSTM cell is used as the final representation [25]. Yang et al. [38] propose re-introducing complementary representation from intermediate layers omitted from the output of the final layer of the transformer by feeding the output of the intermediate layers as individual time steps to a bidirectional GRU and recombining the output of the output of the GRU with the output of the final layer of the transformer [38].

3 The COMBERT Model

3.1 Problem Definition

Figure 1 shows an overview of our proposed approach. Let $U = \{u_1, u_2, ..u_{|U|}\}$ denote a set of users, $I = \{i_1, i_2, ..i_{|I|}\}$ a set of items, and a sequence $S^u = \left(s_1^u, s_2^u, ..s_{|S^u|}^u\right)$ denote the interaction sequence in chronological order for a user $u \in U$ where $S_i^u \in I$. Given $S^{u'} = \left(s_0^{u'}, s_1^{u'}, ..., s_t^{u'}\right) t \geq 1$, an in-progress inter-

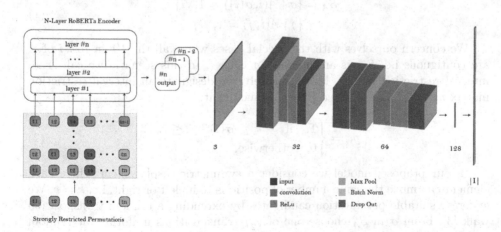

Fig. 1. Overview of our proposed model COMBERT.

action sequence belonging to user u, the objective is to predict the next item $s_{t+1}^{u'} \in I$.

3.2 Data Augmentation

The objective of data augmentation in this work is to serve as the first of a two-stage process to recover and amplify item relation signals via self-supervised pretraining. We aim to generate synthetic UHI from observed UHI samples while preserving the local (subsequence level) and global (full sequence level) context of the observed sample. This use of data augmentation in SR is markedly different from current CL approaches. In CL, the goal of data augmentation is to project UHI into different views and learn item representations by maximizing the agreement between different views of the same UHI in latent space. Current approaches to SR either employ random deletions and subsequence shuffling [35] or substituting and inserting correlated items [16], which leads to context distortion. In our approach, we seek to augment the input sequence without distorting the local or overall context of the sequence. We propose an approach using Strongly Restricted Permutations (SRP) that minimizes changes in the local and global context of the input sequence.

Bounded Interval Restricted Permutations. A class of permutations in which the positions of the elements in a sequence after the permutation are restricted can be specified by a $n \times n$ $(0,1) - matrix$ $A = (a_{ij})$ where is the set of permitted values of $\sigma(i)$, such that:

$$a_{ij} = \begin{cases} 1, & \text{if element } i \text{ can move to position } j. \\ 0, & \text{otherwise.} \end{cases}$$

Let

$$\begin{aligned} S_A &= \{\sigma \mid A(i, \sigma(i)) = 1, \forall i\} \\ S_{(i)} &= \{j \mid A(i,j) = 1, \forall i\} \end{aligned} \tag{1}$$

We concern ourselves with the special cases where all the $1's$ in row i of A are contiguous i.e. $S_{(i)}$ is an interval for each i. In this scenario we call A an interval restriction matrix. More concisely, we designate an interval restriction matrix $n \times n$ $(0,1) - matrix$ $P = (p_{ij})$ such that:

$$p_{ij} = \begin{cases} 1, & \text{if } -k \le \sigma(i) - i \le r. \\ 0, & \text{otherwise.} \end{cases} \tag{2}$$

In our proposed model we consider a symmetric displacement where each element can move the same number of positions to its left or right, i.e. $k = r$. We generate suitable permutation candidates by extending a random transposition walk [3]. From σ in S_A choose one of $\binom{n}{2}$ transpositions uniformly at random and transform σ by switching the two chosen labels. If this new permutation is in S_A, the walk moves there. If not, the walk stays at σ. This results in a

---

Algorithm 1. Random Transposition Walk

Require: sequence S, displacement d, number of permutations to return $\#p$, number of candidate permutations to generate $\#c$

$n \leftarrow |S|$
$A \leftarrow 0_{nxn}$

for $i \in \{1, \ldots, n\}$ **do**
   for $j \in \{1, \ldots, n\}$ **do**
      if $| i - j | \leq d$ **then**
         $a_{ij} \leftarrow 1$
      end if
   end for
end for

$Out \leftarrow \{\}$
$Candidates \leftarrow \{\}$
$C \leftarrow S$

while $| Candidates | \leq \#c$ **do**
   $i_1, i_2 \leftarrow \text{SAMPLE} ([1 \cdots n] , 2)$

   if $\sigma(i_1) \in S_A$ AND $\sigma(i_2) \in S_A$ **then**
      $C \leftarrow \text{SWAP} (C, i_1, i_2)$
      $Candidates \leftarrow \text{Candidates} \cup C$
   end if
end while

$Out \leftarrow \text{SAMPLE} (Candidates , \#p)$

---

symmetric connected Markov chain which has uniform stationary distribution on S_A. Our complete procedure is presented in Algorithm 1.

3.3 Transformer-Based Encoder

Our objective is to deepen the contextualized embeddings extracted from a transformer based encoder. Recent works have demonstrated that richer representations can be learned from transformer encoders by utilizing intermediate transformer layers and not relying solely on the output from the final layer [38].

For the transformer encoder, we employ RoBERTa [15], that is based on the popular BERT model [5]. RoBERTa, among its many enhancements does not utilize next sentence prediction (NSP) which while beneficial in training language models is not applicable in our setting. We replace RoBERTa's byte-level tokenizer with a word-level tokenizer. This modification is necessary because in sequential recommendation every token represents a unique item that must be present in a token vocabulary. The tokens are represented by arbitrary labels and the character representations of the labels do not encode any relationship between the tokens as would occur between words in a language model.

For each dataset, we pre-train a RoBERTa encoder from scratch using only the train set data plus ten SRP augmentations per UHI. It is worthwhile to note that while the pre-training is performed on only the training set, we also pre-train a word-level tokenizer from scratch on the entire dataset so that the entire vocabulary is available to the model when we encode data from the evaluation and test data set. We pad individual sequences to a fixed maximum length in order to obtain a fixed size representation from the encoder after pre-training. More formally, given a sequence $Q = \{q_1, \cdots q_n\}$, we obtain a representation $R \in \mathbb{R}^{t * n * d}$ Where t is the number of layers of the transformer encoder, n is the sequence length and d is the hidden dimension of the transformer.

3.4   Representation Learning with CNNs

Here we describe our CNN architecture which is shown in Fig. 1. The input to the CNN is the representation $R \in \mathbb{R}^{3 * n * d}$ derived from the Transformer encoder. We use the outputs of the final three layers which are treated as separate channels of the input. The initial convolutional layer of the CNN with 3 input channels and 32 output channels comprises a sequential arrangement of 7×7 2D convolutional filter followed by a Leakyrelu layer [36], a 2D max-pooling layer with a 2×2 kernel, a batch normalization layer and finally a dropout layer. The second convolutional layer of the layer of the CNN is identical to the first except it takes 32 input channels and outputs 64.

The resulting output of the second convolutional layer is flattened into a 1D vector to which we apply dropout before passing to a first Feedforward Network (FFN) consisting of a fully connected linear layer with RELU and batch normalization in that order. The output of the first FFN is a compact vector representation of size 128. An additional dropout is applied to the compact representation before passing it to a second FFN comprising a fully connected linear layer, RELU and batch normalization.

4   Experiments

Here, we present our experiments in detail including datasets and associated pre-processing steps, evaluation metrics, compared baselines and our results. We aim to answer the following research questions:

- **RQ1** How does COMBERT perform on sequential recommendation compared to existing SOTA models?
- **RQ2** What is the contribution of the proposed SRP data augmentation approach to the overall performance of COMBERT?
- **RQ3** Can existing SOTA models for sequential recommendation benefit from our proposed data augmentation approach?

4.1   Datasets

We run experiments on seven benchmark sequential recommendation datasets. The datasets span a multiplicity of domains including music, movies, restaurants and events. Exploring a variety of sequential data allows us to investigate the efficacy of our approach on diverse context structures.

- **AOTM:** The AOTM dataset was collected from the Art-of-the-Mix platform and is publicly available. The data set contains $306,830$ listening events, $91,166$ tracks and $21,888$ sessions [17].
- **30MUSIC:** is a collection of listening and playlists data retrieved from Internet radio stations through Last.fm API. The data set contains $638,933$ listening events, $210,633$ items and $37,333$ sessions [29].
- **NOWPLAYING:** Music listening behavior of users created from mining information from social networks. The dataset currently comprises 49 million listening events, $144,011$ artists, $1,346,203$ tracks and $4,150,615$ users [40].
- **YELP:** This dataset is a subset of Yelp's businesses, reviews, and user data. It contains $8,021,122$ reviews about businesses across 8 metropolitan areas in the USA and Canada [39].
- **4SQUARE:** This dataset includes long-term (about 18 months from April 2012 to September 2013) global-scale check-in data collected from Foursquare. It contains $33,278,683$ checkins by 266,909 users on $3,680,126$ venues (in 415 cities in 77 countries). Those 415 cities are the most checked 415 cities in the world, each of which contains at least 10000 check-ins) [37].
- **MovieLens 25M:** This dataset (ml-25m) describes 5-star rating and free-text tagging activity from MovieLens, a movie recommendation service. It contains $25,000,095$ ratings across $62,423$ movies. These data were created by $162,541$ users between January 09, 1995 and November 21, 2019. This dataset was generated on November 21, 2019 [20].
- **LASTFM 1K:** This dataset contains <user, timestamp, artist, song> tuples collected from Last.fm API.This dataset represents the whole listening habits (till May, 5th 2009) for nearly $1,000$ users. he dataset contains 19 million listening events, $176,948$ artists, $1,500,659$ tracks and 992 users [14].

4.2   Pre-Processing

For all datasets, we process the data to get a list of $<user, item, timestamp>$ tuples. The resulting list is sorted from least recent to most recent. A unique ordered list is created for the subset of tuples belonging to each user. We designate the final item in the list as the output; the rest of the list constitutes the input sequence. We create a set of items (vocabulary) for all the items that appear in the input sequence and output. The cardinality of this set gives both the input and output dimension without embedding. To enable our model to fit on a single GPU. We drop items that appear less than 0.005% of total events to reduce the input and output dimension. We also constrain the maximum length of the input sequence to 200 items for the same reason. Table 1 summarize dataset characteristics after pre-processing. We split the input-output pairs

Table 1. Dataset statistics (after pre-processing)

Dataset	#users	#items	#interactions
ML25M	130,004	7,984	8,895,228
4SQUARE	227,301	14,153	7,183,758
YELP	478,630	7,239	2,714,935
LASTFM-1k	414,854	13,430	5,242,483
30M	22,162	2,026	243,428
NOWPLAYING	19,558	1,726	173,465
AOTM	12,670	1,094	83,571

according to a 60/20/20 ratio where 60% of the data is used for training, 20% of the data is used for training validation and 20% of the data is used for testing.

4.3 Evaluation Metrics

MRR. The Reciprocal Rank (RR) information retrieval measure calculates the reciprocal of the rank at which the first relevant document was retrieved. RR is 1 if a relevant document was retrieved at rank 1, if not it is 0.5 if a relevant document was retrieved at rank 2 and so on. When averaged across queries, the measure is called the Mean Reciprocal Rank (MRR). The MRR is defined as the mean of the inverse rank of the first correct answer, taken over all n questions.

$$MRR = \frac{1}{n} \sum_{i=1}^{n} RR_i \qquad (3)$$

The score for an individual question i is the reciprocal rank r_i where the first correct answer appeared.

$$RR_i = \frac{1}{r_i} \qquad (4)$$

Recall. In information retrieval, recall is the fraction of the relevant documents that are successfully retrieved.

$$Recall = \frac{tp}{tp + fn} \qquad (5)$$

We evaluate the performance of our model compared to other baselines MRR@20 and Recall@20.

4.4 Compared Baselines

We compare our proposed model against 4 SOTA SR approaches. It is important to note that our approach is purely sequential i.e. we do not utilize any additional information outside of the ordered list of items for training and recommendation. A brief description of the baseline approaches is provided below.

Table 2. Results for **MRR@20**. Bold face indicates the best results, underline indicates runner up and ties are marked with *.

		30M	NOWP	AOTM	YELP	LASTFM-1K	ML25M	4SQUARE
GRU4REC	w/o SRP	0.143	0.184	0.021	0.015	0.095	0.023	0.146
	w/SRP	0.169	0.186	0.022	0.022	0.118	0.024	0.143
	% Δ	18.18%	1.09%	4.76%	46.67%	24.21%	4.35%	−2.05%
CASER	w/o SRP	0.171	0.193	<u>0.026</u>	0.02	0.157	0.029	<u>0.18</u>
	w/SRP	0.141	**0.235***	0.023	0.018	0.167	<u>0.033</u>	0.176
	% Δ	−17.54%	21.76%	−11.54%	−10.00%	6.37%	13.79%	−2.22%
BERT4REC	w/o SRP	0.133	0.136	0.02	0.011	0.093	0.02	0.122
	w/SRP	0.162	0.184	0.021	<u>0.027</u>	**0.189***	0.023	0.166
	% Δ	21.80%	35.29%	5.00%	145.45%	103.23%	15.00%	36.07%
SASREC	w/o SRP	0.104	0.137	0.02	0.012	0.06	0.02	0.122
	w/SRP	<u>0.175</u>	0.18	0.019	0.018	0.169	0.021	0.167
	% Δ	68.27%	31.39%	−5.00%	50.00%	181.67%	5.00%	36.89%
COMBERT	w/o SRP	0.19	0.188	0.021	0.015	0.138	0.038	**0.214***
	w/SRP	**0.236**	**0.237***	**0.042**	**0.038**	**0.19***	**0.044**	**0.213***
	% Δ	24.21%	26.06%	100.00%	153.33%	37.68%	15.79%	−0.47%

- <u>GRU4REC</u> models UHI with GRU and specialized loss functions for SR [10]
- <u>CASER</u> uses CNN to capture high-order Markov Chains by applying convolutional operations on the embedding matrix of UHI [27]
- <u>BERT4REC</u> models UHI with a Transformer and trains via Cloze task [26]
- <u>SASREC</u> uses a left-to-right self-attention to model UHI [12]

4.5   RQ1

From Tables 2 and 5, we observe that COMBERT, our proposed model, outperforms existing baselines on all seven datasets. Tables 3 and 4 show the performance improvement of COMBERT over the baseline models for MRR and

Table 3. MRR@20 baseline comparison

	GRU4REC	CASER	BERT4REC	SASREC
30M	65.03%	38.01%	77.44%	126.92%
NOWP	28.80%	22.80%	74.26%	72.99%
AOTM	100.00%	61.54%	110.00%	110.00%
YELP	153.33%	90.00%	245.45%	216.67%
LASTFM-1K	100.00%	21.02%	104.30%	216.67%
ML25M	91.30%	51.72%	120.00%	120.00%
4SQUARE	45.89%	18.33%	74.59%	74.59%
Average	**83.48%**	**43.35%**	**115.15%**	**133.98%**

Table 4. RECALL@20 baseline comparison

	GRU4REC	CASER	BERT4REC	SASREC
30M	64.39%	38.91%	115.57%	159.66%
NOWP	38.17%	33.81%	134.67%	119.25%
AOTM	69.14%	48.91%	98.55%	77.92%
YELP	101.54%	63.75%	142.59%	147.17%
LASTFM-1K	88.17%	20.27%	86.17%	196.61%
ML25M	63.83%	43.93%	79.07%	81.18%
4SQUARE	27.23%	11.47%	47.72%	52.35%
Average	**64.64%**	**37.29%**	**100.62%**	**119.16%**

RECALL respectively. The average performance improvement across all the baselines is 94% for MRR and 80% for Recall. Surprisingly, the next best performing model is CASER, a CNN based model, followed by GRU4REC a pioneering deep learning model for SR. In our experiments, the recently proposed self-attention based models SASREC and BERT4REC without data augmentation were the worst performing models. These findings merit further investigation as they appear inconsistent with the recent literature. One possible explanation is the difference in approaches to measuring SR performance employed by different authors. In our experiments, we do not modify the input sequences and merely hold out the last item for prediction. Our MRR and RECALL values reported are thus based solely on the final item that is held out.

4.6   RQ2

Tables 3 and 4 show the performance improvement of COMBERT over the baseline models for MRR and RECALL respectively. The average performance improvement across all the baselines is 94% for MRR and 80% for Recall. We observe that the average performance improvement in MRR drops by 39% from 94% to 55% when we apply our SRP data augmentation technique to the training data for the baselines. A similar drop of 37% is observed for average Recall improvement after training data augmentation. In our own proposed model, we perform an ablation study which omits the data augmentation step and observe a 51% drop in average MRR and 35% drop in Recall. These observations taken together strongly suggest that our proposed SRP data augmentation strategy is a strong contributor to the overall performance of our SR model. It also confirms works from NLP that BERT encoders are able to learn superior contextualized token representations.

4.7   RQ3

Table 6 shows the average improvement across datasets of the compared baselines after our data augmentation technique was applied to the training dataset.

Table 5. Results for **RECALL@20**. Bold face indicates the best results, underline indicates runner up and ties are marked with *.

		30M	NOWP	AOTM	YELP	LASTFM-1K	ML25M	4SQUARE
GRU4REC	w/o SRP	0.278	0.338	0.081	0.065	0.186	0.094	0.382
	w/SRP	0.326	0.351	0.079	0.085	0.233	0.092	0.378
	% Δ	17.27%	3.85%	−2.47%	30.77%	25.27%	−2.13%	−1.05%
CASER	w/o SRP	<u>0.329</u>	0.349	<u>0.092</u>	0.08	0.291	0.107	<u>0.436</u>
	w/SRP	0.282	<u>0.427</u>	0.091	0.072	0.317	<u>0.12</u>	0.426
	% Δ	−14.29%	22.35%	−1.09%	−10.00%	8.93%	12.15%	−2.29%
BERT4REC	w/o SRP	0.212	0.199	0.069	0.054	0.188	0.086	0.329
	w/SRP	0.301	0.333	0.081	<u>0.097</u>	<u>0.341</u>	0.091	0.398
	% Δ	41.98%	67.34%	17.39%	79.63%	81.38%	5.81%	20.97%
SASREC	w/o SRP	0.176	0.213	0.077	0.053	0.118	0.085	0.319
	w/SRP	0.326	0.34	0.078	0.077	0.317	0.089	0.394
	% Δ	85.23%	59.62%	1.30%	45.28%	168.64%	4.71%	23.51%
COMBERT	w/o SRP	0.381	0.376	0.074	0.068	0.315	0.141	0.459
	w/SRP	**0.457**	**0.467**	**0.137**	**0.131**	**0.35**	**0.154**	**0.486**
	% Δ	19.95%	24.20%	85.14%	92.65%	11.11%	9.22%	5.88%

Table 6. Average baseline improvement with SRP

	GRU4REC	CASER	BERT4REC	SASREC
MRR@20	13.89%	0.09%	51.69%	52.60%
RECALL@20	10.22%	2.25%	44.93%	55.47%

With the exception of CASER, all the baseline models enjoyed an appreciable performance boost in both MRR and RECALL. The most significant gains were observed in SASREC and BERT4REC, two models that employ Transformer based Self-Attention for item representation learning. We observe a greater than 50% average performance boost in MRR and RECALL for those models. We also see a significant boost in GRU4REC, an RNN based model that does not employ an attention mechanism. CASER, a CNN based model was mostly unaffected by our data augmentation approach. It only registered a negligible improvement in RECALL while the average MRR across datasets was virtually unchanged. Overall the results from Table 6 suggest that our data augmentation approach can be applied to the spectrum of SR models without any significant risk of performance degradation and will likely contribute performance gains especially for models utilizing self-attention.

5 Conclusion

In this work we have proposed a two stage technique to recover and amplify item relation signals which are compromised in training data for SR due to limitations of the underlying candidate generation process from which the training data is obtained. In the first stage, we recover compromised signals with a novel data augmentation process that involves generating synthetic UHI from observed UHI samples while preserving local and global sequence level contextual information of observed samples. In the second stage we employ a self-supervised pre-training approach that leverages the recovered item relation signals to learn superior item representations. We develop a novel CNN-based SR model as a downstream task to utilize our learned item representations. Extensive experiments on seven benchmark datasets for next-item recommendations demonstrate that our approach is able to recover item relational dynamics distorted by the candidate generation process. Our proposed SR model significantly outperforms four SOTA models for SR and an ablation study confirms that our item representation learning approach is a significant contributor to the models superior performance. Additionally, we find that the majority of our compared SOTA baselines also enjoy a significant performance boost from utilizing our learned item representations. In the future, we would like to extend this work to explore the properties of item relation signals that are recovered/recoverable and neural approaches to optimize item relation signal recovery.

References

1. Amankwata, B., Fletcher, K.K.: Contexts embedding for sequential service recommendation. In: 2022 IEEE 46th Annual Computers, Software, and Applications Conference (COMPSAC), pp. 1087–1092. IEEE (2022)
2. Bahdanau, D., Cho, K., Bengio, Y.: Neural machine translation by jointly learning to align and translate. CoRR abs/1409.0473 (2015)
3. Blumberg, O.: Permutations with interval restrictions. Ph.D. thesis, PhD thesis, Stanford University (2012)
4. Chen, T., Kornblith, S., Norouzi, M., Hinton, G.E.: A simple framework for contrastive learning of visual representations. ArXiv abs/2002.05709 (2020)
5. Devlin, J., Chang, M.W., Lee, K., Toutanova, K.: Bert: pre-training of deep bidirectional transformers for language understanding. In: NAACL (2019)
6. Fletcher, K.: Regularizing matrix factorization with implicit user preference embeddings for web API recommendation. In: 2019 IEEE International Conference on Services Computing (SCC), pp. 1–8. IEEE (2019)
7. Fletcher, K.K.: A quality-aware web API recommender system for mashup development. In: Ferreira, J.E., Musaev, A., Zhang, L.-J. (eds.) SCC 2019. LNCS, vol. 11515, pp. 1–15. Springer, Cham (2019). https://doi.org/10.1007/978-3-030-23554-3_1
8. Grbovic, M., et al.: E-commerce in your inbox: product recommendations at scale. In: Proceedings of the 21th ACM SIGKDD International Conference on Knowledge Discovery and Data Mining (2015)
9. He, R., McAuley, J.: Fusing similarity models with markov chains for sparse sequential recommendation. In: 2016 IEEE 16th International Conference on Data Mining (ICDM), pp. 191–200 (2016)
10. Hidasi, B., Karatzoglou, A., Baltrunas, L., Tikk, D.: Session-based recommendations with recurrent neural networks. CoRR abs/1511.06939 (2016)
11. Hidasi, B., Quadrana, M., Karatzoglou, A., Tikk, D.: Parallel recurrent neural network architectures for feature-rich session-based recommendations. In: Proceedings of the 10th ACM Conference on Recommender Systems (2016)

12. Kang, W.C., McAuley, J.: Self-attentive sequential recommendation. In: 2018 IEEE International Conference on Data Mining (ICDM), pp. 197–206 (2018)
13. Kwapong, B.A., Anarfi, R., Fletcher, K.K.: Personalized service recommendation based on user dynamic preferences. In: Ferreira, J.E., Musaev, A., Zhang, L.-J. (eds.) SCC 2019. LNCS, vol. 11515, pp. 77–91. Springer, Cham (2019). https://doi.org/10.1007/978-3-030-23554-3_6
14. Lastfm: Last.fm   dataset   -   1k   users.   http://ocelma.net/MusicRecommendationDataset/lastfm-1K.html. Accessed 30 Dec 2020
15. Liu, Y., et al.: Roberta: a robustly optimized Bert pretraining approach. ArXiv abs/1907.11692 (2019)
16. Liu, Z., Chen, Y.G., Li, J., Yu, P.S., McAuley, J., Xiong, C.: Contrastive self-supervised sequential recommendation with robust augmentation. ArXiv abs/2108.06479 (2021)
17. McFee, B., Lanckriet, G.: The natural language of playlists. In: ISMIR (2011)
18. Miaschi, A., Dell'Orletta, F.: Contextual and non-contextual word embeddings: an in-depth linguistic investigation. In: REPL4NLP (2020)
19. Mikolov, T., Chen, K., Corrado, G.S., Dean, J.: Efficient estimation of word representations in vector space. In: ICLR (2013)
20. MovieLense: Movielens 25m dataset. https://grouplens.org/datasets/movielens/25m/. Accessed 30 Dec 2020
21. Pennington, J., Socher, R., Manning, C.D.: Glove: global vectors for word representation. In: EMNLP (2014)
22. Rendle, S., Freudenthaler, C., Schmidt-Thieme, L.: Factorizing personalized markov chains for next-basket recommendation. In: WWW 2010 (2010)
23. Sahlgren, M., Holst, A., Kanerva, P.: Permutations as a means to encode order in word space (2008)
24. Song, Y., Lee, J.: Augmenting recurrent neural networks with high-order user-contextual preference for session-based recommendation. ArXiv abs/1805.02983 (2018)
25. Song, Y., Wang, J., Liang, Z., Liu, Z., Jiang, T.: Utilizing Bert intermediate layers for aspect based sentiment analysis and natural language inference. ArXiv abs/2002.04815 (2020)
26. Sun, F., et al.: Bert4rec: sequential recommendation with bidirectional encoder representations from transformer. In: Proceedings of the 28th ACM International Conference on Information and Knowledge Management (2019)
27. Tang, J., Wang, K.: Personalized top-n sequential recommendation via convolutional sequence embedding. In: Proceedings of the Eleventh ACM International Conference on Web Search and Data Mining (2018)
28. Tian, Y., Sun, C., Poole, B., Krishnan, D., Schmid, C., Isola, P.: What makes for good views for contrastive learning. ArXiv abs/2005.10243 (2020)
29. Turrin, R., Quadrana, M., Condorelli, A., Pagano, R., Cremonesi, P.: 30music listening and playlists dataset. In: RecSys Posters (2015)
30. Vasile, F., Smirnova, E., Conneau, A.: Meta-prod2vec: Product embeddings using side-information for recommendation. In: Proceedings of the 10th ACM Conference on Recommender Systems (2016)
31. Vaswani, A.,et al.: Attention is all you need. In: NIPS (2017)
32. Wu, J., et al.: Self-supervised graph learning for recommendation. In: Proceedings of the 44th International ACM SIGIR Conference on Research and Development in Information Retrieval (2021)

33. Wu, J., Cai, R., Wang, H.: Déjà vu: a contextualized temporal attention mechanism for sequential recommendation. In: Proceedings of The Web Conference 2020 (2020)
34. Wu, S., Tang, Y., Zhu, Y., Wang, L., Xie, X., Tan, T.: Session-based recommendation with graph neural networks. In: AAAI (2019)
35. Xie, X., Sun, F., Liu, Z., Gao, J., Ding, B., Cui, B.: Contrastive pre-training for sequential recommendation. ArXiv abs/2010.14395 (2020)
36. Xu, B., Wang, N., Chen, T., Li, M.: Empirical evaluation of rectified activations in convolutional network. ArXiv abs/1505.00853 (2015)
37. Yang, D., Zhang, D., Zheng, V., Yu, Z.: Modeling user activity preference by leveraging user spatial temporal characteristics in LBSNs. IEEE Trans. Syst. Man, Cybern. Syst. **45**, 129–142 (2015)
38. Yang, J., Zhao, H.: Deepening hidden representations from pre-trained language models for natural language understanding. ArXiv abs/1911.01940 (2019)
39. Yelp: The dataset. https://www.yelp.com/dataset. Accessed 30 Dec 2020
40. Zangerle, E., Pichl, M., Gassler, W., Specht, G.: nowplaying music dataset: Extracting listening behavior from twitter. In: WISMM 2014 (2014)

Defending Environmental Competence: A Moral Principle for Data Use

Zhao Li[✉], Wen Wang, Honggui He, and Jingyi Cui

Law School, Jiangxi University of Finance and Economics, Nanchang 330013, Jiangxi Province, China
johnleehust@hotmail.com

Abstract. While data use promotes industrial upgrading and creates new values, it also causes many moral risks, such as algorithm discrimination, seamless monitoring and privacy invasion. In order to resolve these crises, various countries have initially established some ethical principles and frameworks in this field. It's time to move from principles and frameworks to ethical data use practices. But integrating the principles of AI ethical framework into the public governance system without discrimination may cause excessive constraints on the use of data especially by enterprises, so as to inhibit the creative production of data value by various subjects and hinder the orderly development of digital economy. This study constructs a most general moral principle in the digital era with the purpose of maintaining environmental competence for data use. With this moral principle, legislators and public policy makers may find a way to guide the data use behavior of enterprises and public institutions towards the direction of human prosperity, and well balance the order and freedom.

Keywords: Data use · Moral principle · Environmental competence

1 Introduction

While data creates huge economic value, it also brings unprecedented moral risks. Issues such as algorithmic bias, derogation of human dignity, privacy evasion, responsibility anomie, marginalization of human participation and decision-making [1] are threatening the social order of various countries. Irresponsible data use is an important factor in this kind of threat. In order to avoid the derogation of people's subjectivity caused by data use and prevent technology from being lost, we must always defend the moral and ethical principles, to keep data use in a human-centered way [2].

Many countries and organizations have issued ethical policies related to data use. China's New Generation of AI Governance Specialized Committee issued the principles of New Generation AI Governance-Development of responsible Artificial Intelligence, which established eight principles for AI development, including harmony and friendship, fairness and justice, inclusiveness and sharing, respect for privacy, security and control, shared responsibility, open cooperation, and agile governance. According to Data Security Law of China stipulates, carrying out data processing or developing new

W. Qingyang and L.-J. Zhang (Eds.): SCC 2022, LNCS 13738, pp. 41–55, 2022.
https://doi.org/10.1007/978-3-031-23515-3_4

data technologies should be conducive to promoting economic and social development, as well as enhancing people's well-being, and in line with social morality and ethics" [3]. To implement these principles of data use, it is necessary to integrate them into public governance system in form of law or policies [4].

But the opening, sharing and utilization of data is the prerequisite for the prosperity of digital economy. Only when data could be circulated and used freely, people could use data in a creative way. The existing legal systems of various countries have promulgated special legal frameworks to regulate the data flow and use of data. Although these frameworks are far from meeting the ethical requirements, they have already imposed a certain degree of restrictions on data use by enterprises and public institutions. Sufficient caution is needed when we attempt to add a new constraint to the existing legal framework. If we extract some principles from existing ethical framework of data use or AI to take into enforcement without deliberation, it may cause too many constrains on data use, down to restrain the creative production of data value by various subjects and hinder the orderly development of digital economy.

It is not appropriate to integrate the moral principles of data use and the principles of AI ethical framework into the public governance system without discrimination. That too many moral principles squeeze into public governance will lead to the improper expansion of regulatory power. Since freedom of conduct can only be restricted by freedom itself, moral principles can only be developed from the morality of data use (and thus necessarily from the intrinsic nature the behavior). The principle to be integrated into the structure of public governance previously must be the most general moral principle in the digital age. Based on the equal dignity and liberty of human beings, this study demonstrates one of the most general moral principles in the digital age, and further clarifies the content of the critical moral principle for data use with the purpose of defending of environmental competence for individuals according to it. With this moral principle, legislators and public policy makers may find a way to guide the data use behavior of enterprises and public institutions towards the direction of human prosperity, and well balance the order and freedom.

2 Research Objects and Basic Concepts

The term data use discussed in this study refers to the behavior of using data in a networked and intelligent way. In this sense, to discuss data use, we need to pay attention to the following aspects:

(1) The background of the digital age. Traditionally, the collection and processing of sensitive personal information by enterprises or other institutions will lead to serious moral crisis, which can be solved in the legal and ethical framework of privacy. This study only focuses on the impact and challenges caused by data use to the current order under the background of digitalization, networking, and intelligence.
(2) This term includes a variety of technical means. At present, many related literatures worked with this topic under the term ethical principles for artificial intelligence, but the principles discussed in this study involve more general types of technology. In addition to AI, big data, cloud computing, Internet, blockchain, virtual/augmented

reality and other technologies are also technical means which might cause ethical or moral crisis in the digital age.

(3) It covers multiple sessions of data processing. China's Data Security Law defines data use as one session in data processing, which is tied to collection, storage, processing, transmission, provision, and disclosure. This kind of classification is the result of adopting the terms in the technical process into the legal text directly by the legislator. Compared with the technical process, the discussion on whether the behavior is ethical or match up to moral principles focuses on the nature and influence of the behavior. In daily language (rather than technical language), the extension of the term "use" is much broader than processing, which will not focus on the technical process and can more naturally point to the nature and influence of the technology, The so-called concept of data use in this paper covers collection, storage, processing, transmission and other technical sessions related to data value production.

In addition, the research object is morality of data use rather than ethics of it. Morality is the conduct established by the subject according to his or her own internal been, while ethics refers to the real world and its order [5]. To explore the internal requirements and rules of enterprises in the practice of data use is to establish the internal spiritual integrity of the main body, so it is more accurate in the name of morality. To explore the internal requirements and rules of enterprises in the practice of data use is to establish the internal spiritual integrity of the subject, so it is more accurate to define it as morality. In AI and other related fields, the existing literature and policies commonly use the ethical framework, which refers to the practice rules that enterprises and other subjects still need to follow outside the existing legal framework.

The reason is that, on the one hand, such a framework is realistic due to the establishment of authoritative institutions; On the other hand, the principle included in the framework is not completely out of the inherent requirements of the subject behavior itself. This study is based on the ethical framework as a reference, by refining the internal requirements of the practice of the main body, and ultimately on data use morality. This is because, on the one hand, such a framework is positive due to the formulation of authoritative institutions. On the other hand, the principles included in the framework are not entirely out of the inherent requirements of the subject. This study takes the ethical framework as a reference, refines the inherent requirements of practice of the subject, then finally concentrates on the moral principle of data use.

3   A Critical Rule of Morality for Data Use

To conceptualize the morality of data use, the first step is to put forward and demonstrate the general moral principle of data use. This principle can be temporarily expressed as: data use cannot inhibit or hinder the operation of essentially different internal regulations in different social aspects. The function of this principle is to provide a critical reference for revising the real morality of a particular society, as well as abandoning, and adjusting customary rules. This kind of morality is not developed from specific policy objectives or ethical framework, but from the most general moral requirements. The content of this moral principle can be demonstrated by amending the principle of equal liberty. Under the evaluation of this moral principle, the most fundamental threat brings up by the data use can be identified. The specific analysis and demonstration are as follows.

3.1 From Transcendental Subject to Daily Life

Modern thinkers usually often trace the most general principle back to the self-legislation of individuals in its purity. According to Kant's theory, man is a kind of equally free and rational being. This moral principle is the highest regulation established by rational individuals in a simple form [6]. After excluding the provisions given by experience such as education, constitution, nature and moral emotion, rational individuals develop the most general moral norms in a simple form according to their own purpose and universalization requirements. That is, everyone should never regard himself and all other rational beings merely as Means but always treat others as end at any time [7].

If all the heteronomy from experience is removed, everyone will accept such an institutional arrangement in society:

(1) Everyone enjoys an equal system of fundamental freedoms; (2) the basic freedom system of all people should fill the whole legal space, so as far as this particular society is concerned, overall freedom is the most extensive. These two points basically constitute the principle of equality and freedom in the basic structure of Rawls' society (the first principle of justice). Under the condition that the veil of ignorance shields all knowledge of heteronomy, this principle is the choice of rational individuals purely out of self-discipline. In Kant's view, although moral practice needs to exclude any rational speculation of empirical materials, it needs to be guided by ideas (as the substantive purpose) [8], but this kind of metaphysical substantive concept cannot be proved by human reason [9] and cannot form knowledge.

However, Kant's ethical principles are far from enough to regulate the use of enterprise data. Along this theoretical approach, as long as the data information used by enterprises is informed and agreed by users, or through anonymous processing, they can enter the field of free use, free from the constraints of moral laws. For the current ethical requirements for the use of enterprise data, this rule is too narrow. The reason lies in the one-sided emphasis on the status relationship and expression of will between subjects, and the lack of attention to the relationship between subjects and society. Because of the transcendental nature of Kant's presupposed cognitive subject, the moral principles proposed at the theoretical thinking level must be alienated from social conditions. In the practice of people's daily life, the subject and social conditions are always closely intertwined. If we want to refine the moral principles in the relationship between the subject and social conditions, we must abandon Kant's transcendental cognitive subject, and refine the moral principles for the use of enterprise data from the practice of people's daily life.

3.2 The Most General Critical Morality

The second step is to refine the specific content of critical morality from the practice of people's daily life. Taking daily practice (rather than abstract theoretical thinking) as the premise, we cannot search for moral principles in an abstract way but need to appeal to the intuition of people's daily experience. In daily experience, people can always acquire a great deal of knowledge. The knowledge gained in practice (such as the most convenient way to commute, the effective way to comfort friends, the order of tidying up the room, etc.) has not been clarified in theory, but it can provide effective guidance for human practice in various fields. In the pragmatic philosophers James, Dewey and Peirce, the knowledge in experience is highly valued. The British ideologist Oakeshott found that although the knowledge gained directly from experience has not been reflected on the theoretical level, it already includes judgments and decisions on what to do, what should be done, what to do well, what to do is important and how to do it [10].

However, different from the assumptions of pragmatism philosophy, these judgments and decisions are not purely independent creations and inventions, but out of the pro-visions and restrictions of responsibility in various social fields. In this sense, people's judgments and decisions are developed from the norms in the social field. If we put aside the details of these judgments and decisions, can we grasp the most general norms that cover all human experience? If we insist on extracting norms from the practice of daily life, we will find that the norms that guide people in the complex responsibility network are diverse. No one can thoroughly clarify the contents of these norms in theory. But theoretical thinking can grasp the differences between internal norms in different social fields and clarify the diversity of these rules. In daily life, People can recognize that they are not acting within a single normative framework of the same nature. Economic, political, social, aesthetic, and ethical fields have their own unique internal regulations. Based on this understanding, people should not confuse different types of regulations in practice, for example, they can't regulate people's actions in the political field according to the inherent requirements of the economic field, nor can they manage the family in the way of managing the company. Therefore, at the social level, the most general critical morality can be expressed as: the particularity of internal provisions in different fields should be generally recognized, respected, and maintained.

3.3 The Critical Morality for Data Use

The third step is to clarify critical morality in the special scenarios of data use. Outside the framework of the traditional right to privacy, people pay attention to the regulation of the use of data because since the 1960s, civil computers have begun to have the ability to deal with large amounts of data. As the concern expressed by American writer Vance Packard, automatic data processing through computer technology threatens not only privacy, but also many other rights [11] (such as the development of one's own unique personality and endowment, etc.). It leads to many problems, including algorithmic discrimination, consumption monitoring, decision guidance, and user portraits.

With the generalization of automatic data processing, the classification logic of computers has gradually become the basic rule of daily life. The vast amounts of data collected from facts by sensors deployed everywhere are captured under elaborate categories and converted into codes to enter the calculation. If there are in-consistencies between real-world experience and the code, prediction-oriented calculations will ignore and exclude data that cannot be included in existing categories in order to bridge this gap [12]. In this process, code rules interfere with or even replace the operation of internal regulations in different fields. With the human governance practice becoming more and more dependent on algorithms, the operation of rules in various fields has been more and more hindered. The particularity and diversity of internal rules also gradually give way to the rules imposed by algorithm engineers from specific social areas and specific situations. To criticize and correct this reality, we must require that the use of data can't restrain or hinder the operation of internal rules in the social field, as the critical morality of the digital society.

4   The Critical Moral Principle for Data Use

The key to connecting critical morality and positive law is the principle of moral criticism. The principle of moral criticism here can be expressed as follows: the use of data cannot develop a wider range of environmental competences for any special individual, organization or social group at the expense of weakening and destroying the environmental competence of others.

As a basic indicator for morally evaluating the use of data, environmental competence consists of three interrelated elements: (1) awareness of the surrounding environment and its impact on itself; (2) awareness of specific goals in this environment in order to achieve specific goals; and (3) responsibility that must be assumed by taking responsibility to use or change the environment to achieve specific goals. (1) and (3) the two elements are included in the American management scientist Steele's definition of environmental competence [13], and the element (2) is a supplementary construction to bridge the gap between environmental awareness and action ability.

The term environment here is reference to a place for individual action and a social medium to show the inherent potential of the individual. Individuals do not create and construct responsibilities through abstract ideas, but in practice, through their own interaction with the environment, encounter the inherent rules of the social field, and develop responsibilities in specific situations and situations in the process of understanding these provisions.

How does the moral critical principle of data use develop from critical morality, and in what way is supported by relevant policies and documents, so as to become a real morality in the field of data use? The specific arguments are as follows:

4.1   From Critical Morality to a Principle

The moral critical principle of digital use is the embodiment of the critical morality of digital society at the individual level. The internal regulations in different areas of experience are not external rules imposed by others, but norms that individuals understand in practice in order to develop specific responsibilities and endowments in practice. In practice, individuals do not apply transcendental rules to the social environment within themselves but participate in the operation of internal regulations in various social fields in the process of interaction with the surrounding environment. Only when the individual is aware of the surrounding environment and the influence it exerts, and in this environment can respond to the internal regulations of different fields, develop the responsibilities that must be undertaken (to achieve specific goals), and be able to assume these responsibilities, use and change environmental settings to promote the achievement of goals, can individuals effectively respond to the inherent provisions of the field of experience. Only in this way, the operation of the internal provisions of the field at the individual level will not be hindered and distorted, so as to realize the requirements of critical morality. Therefore, individuals enjoy the freedom or right to develop environmental competence, which is a natural extension of critical morality at the individual level.

In order to put forward the principle of moral criticism in the digital society, it is necessary to introduce a special social hypothesis to regard society as a mutually beneficial cooperative cause in order to develop the widest range of environmental competences. In order to fully realize the requirements of critical morality, although the society (1) encourages society as a whole to develop the widest range of environmental competences, it must be subject to the following restrictions: (2) each person has an equal right to develop the widest range of environmental competences relative to himself within his or her own endowment; and (3) the environmental competences actually developed by each person need to be compatible with others.

The use of data in a computer context may threaten the moral boundaries of this social cooperation system in special ways. The general aspect of this threat is that (a) if classification logic becomes a necessary condition for people to organize their daily life, it will weaken the ability to achieve self-discipline according to the inherent provisions of the field of experience, allowing other laws such as business goals or administrative injunctions to dominate governance actions based on data use. Among them, the special aspects are: (b) organizations or institutions may improve their own environmental competence at the expense of restraining or weakening the environmental competence of some individuals in the process of using data. In order to deal with this threat, enterprises must abide by the following moral principles in the use of data: the purpose of data use is to promote the development of a wider range of environmental competence of society as a whole, but not at the expense of weakening or impairing the environmental competence already possessed by other individuals, organizations or groups, or inhibiting the development of these subjects' environmental competence.

4.2 Critical Moral Principle in Policies

The principle of moral criticism in the use of data has been supported by policies and reporting documents in relevant fields. The general threat to human environmental competence caused by the use of data in the way of intelligent algorithms has been concerned by the international community. For example, the 2017 report of the French data Protection Agency, how do humans stay in a favorable position: a report on moral problems caused by artificial Intelligence algorithms focuses on issues of general concern in the context of intelligent data processing: how to ensure that the predictions and advice provided by algorithms only support human decisions and actions, rather than causing human beings to no longer take responsibility? The report equates the latter situation with the loss of free will [14]. Artificial Intelligence: Australia's Ethical Framework released by the Australian Department of Industrial Innovation and Technology emphasizes the protection of environmental competence in the principle of people oriented values: artificial intelligence should respect, protect, and promote human rights, achieve diversity, respect human freedom and individual autonomy. The system should be designed to enhance, complement, and empower human cognitive, social, and cultural skills [15]. The Ethical Guide to trusted artificial Intelligence, drafted by the Eu Expert Group on Advanced Artificial Intelligence in 2019, also takes environmental competence as a basic indicator in the basic principles for the protection of human initiative: artificial intelligence systems should empower human beings to make informed decisions and nurture their basic rights, ensure that human beings them-selves, rather than intelligent algorithms, dominate decision-making and judgment [16].

Environmental ability is the key to the development of human endowment, and the threat posed by intelligent algorithms to human development has been widely recognized. The expression of eliminating harm to human development is common in various official documents related to artificial intelligence and intelligent algorithms. For example, the Declaration on artificial Intelligence Ethics in data Protection, issued at the 40th International Conference of the Privacy Commissioner in 2018, states in the fundamental values and principles that call for guarantees: to ensure that artificial intelligence systems are developed in a manner that promotes rather than hinders or endangers human development [17].

In addition to the support of a number of policies, the principle of ethical criticism of the use of data can also complement the shortcomings of the existing legal framework and respond to new problems caused by the use of data. For example, in the take-out rider and digital platform scene, the platform enterprise collects and processes the data of the rider's height, restaurant floor, consumer preference, real-time weather, road section, time, and so on. The results are applied to the management behaviors such as matching rider, estimated time, planning route, spatio-temporal supervision, quantitative performance, etc., at the expense of the rider's autonomy in many aspects. It is subject to strict digital control [18]. Under the evaluation of the principle of moral criticism of the use of data, strict data control, even if it does not help to define complete labor relations, will bear the corresponding responsibility for damaging the rider's environmental ability and causing the use of data beyond reasonable limits.

In addition, in the field of personal information, the rule of informed consent is supposed to be a means for users to restrict the use of enterprise data and participate in joint control. However, through the lack of transparent data processing, enterprises will weaken the environmental ability of individual users and fail the function of informed consent rules. The principle of moral criticism will restrict companies from using algorithms that are difficult to explain, lack transparency, and are not conducive to user access. If digital portraits are used for social sorting and discrimination or decision-making induction, they will not be supported because they endanger the equal rights of individuals in developing environmental competence.

5 Evaluation Indicators of Data Usage Design

Although a social system aimed at developing the broadest range of environmental competence can conceptualize the design indicators used by some data with reference to the principles of moral criticism, these indicators are practical in nature and require public bodies to define specific evaluation rules in specific situations in conjunction with the plans used by the data.

This study briefly discusses the commemorative nature of this index system with reference to several important aspects of the design of data use regulated by the principle of moral criticism. These indicators are: cognitive interest, technology scale, interaction, space limitation and participation. The following analysis is only the initial result of this study, and only carries on the image inspection to this question.

5.1 Cognitive Interest

The destruction of the user's environmental ability caused by the use of data, first of all, may lead to the distortion of people's cognitive interest. According to the definition of German philosopher Appel, cognitive interest is an intrusive world understanding [19] that empirical materials rely on in the process of constructing knowledge, which is independent of human reason. This understanding is diverse. When the main purpose of the cognitive system is productive or the control of the environment, it is essentially functional; when the main interest is to promote the good of society as a whole, the cognitive system is essentially political [20].

In the context of digital society, the concept of cognitive interest covers a wider range of options, involving any bias used to constitute a particular cognition. Products or services developed by enterprises through the use of data often instill certain prejudices into the public who buy products or receive services. In the operation of the search index and the targeted recommendation of the e-commerce platform, the algorithms used to support these services are full of such biases. In the process of using empowered data, digital technology may further lead to the solidification of individual or group cognitive ability and hinder the potential for people to develop cognition according to their own understanding. For example, through the intelligent processing of consumer data, enterprises accurately push advertisements to target users at a specific time and scene to induce their impulsive consumption. This kind of consumption manipulation actually suppresses people's own cognitive interests and possibilities.

The society that is most beneficial to the cultivation of human environmental ability must have a polycentric cognitive system that equally accepts different cognitive interests. Because in order to make the development of human beings' diverse endowments and avoid the inhibition imposed by the social system as far as possible, it is necessary to prevent the solidification of their cognitive interests. For example, when enterprises use data to develop search engines, they need to ensure that every information object has the same opportunity to be included in the search, and that each piece of information has the same chance to be retrieved by users as much as possible. In this way, we can not only reduce the tragedies caused by the bias promoted by Baidu (such as the Wei Jersey incident [21]), but also give full play to the function of digital media by maintaining individual cognition. Therefore, the design of data use needs to accommodate multiple cognitive interest as much as possible. Even if digital products and services are to operate under the support of a single cognitive interest or prejudice, designers should accept the possibility of other cognitive interests for the relevant individuals or groups.

5.2 Size of Technology

Because the technology and behavior of cyberspace can cross the boundaries and obstacles of physical space, the influence of data use far exceeds the market subjects in the industrial era. In this context, the scale of enterprise technology can be extended to the scope of influence of data use. So far, the technical scale of data use has not become the core issue concerned by social system designers. Most enterprises believe in the idea that the bigger the technology, the better.

However, it is often ignored that the situational characteristics of data use are always weakened with the expansion of the scale of technology. When a large number of individuals accept the products and services provided by enterprises based on the use of data on a large technological scale for reasons of convenience, the association and interaction with environmental settings are more likely to be hindered. So, the excessive scale of technology used by data threatens the ability of individuals to develop specific responsibilities from their surroundings and to achieve their goals by mobilizing relevant resources. Therefore, the effectiveness of the interaction between the individual and the environment limits the technical scale of data use.

As the scale of technology is often proportional to the size of enterprise organizations, there have been legislation to limit the size of organizations and indirectly limit the scale of technology used by data. The guidelines for the Classification and Classification of Internet platforms (draft for soliciting opinions), organized and drafted by the State Administration for Market Regulation on October 29, 2021, has more than 500 million annual active users according to standards such as super restrictive capacity and ultra-high economic weight. The core business involves two types of platform business, and a platform with a market capitalization (valuation) of more than 1 trillion yuan is defined as a super platform [22]. The organization released the same day the "Internet platform implementation subject responsibility Guide (draft for soliciting opinions)" on super-large Internet platform operators in equal governance, open ecology, data management and other aspects to impose more stringent responsibilities [23].

At the international level, the California Consumer Privacy Act stipulates that companies subject to the law must have a total annual income of more than $25 million [24]. Or 50000 or more copies of personal information on the basis of individual consumers, individual households or devices are purchased, received, sold or shared at a time or in total each year [25]. This means that the operation of the enterprise or the processing of data to a certain scale, it is necessary to bear special responsibility. This provision has at least indirectly taken into account the technology scale element. At present, it is difficult to use theory to define the appropriate technology scale in a quantitative way, but public institutions need to weaken the negative impact of excessive technology scale through law and various policy means in practice.

5.3 Interactivity

In the context of data use, interactivity refers to the possibility of data-driven products and services to respond to users' judgments and decisions. This not only requires data products and services to consider the user's background, experience, and how they feel during the operation [26], but also helps to give individuals more autonomy and room for thinking. For example, if enterprises can visually let users know why they are recommended through products developed using data, in order to play a more active role in directional push by supporting or changing standards.

Some people think that interactivity needs to be based on accessibility. Accessibility (of data processing media such as intelligent algorithms) enables users to understand the way enterprises process data and gain greater autonomy in interacting with intelligent products and services. Unfortunately, most people cannot understand the source code of intelligent algorithms.

In contrast, testability, that is, the degree to which the system supports users to test it [27], is a better practical indicator for developing interactive designs. In the environment settings constructed by digital products and services, the design with good testability can enhance human understanding and control. Suppose a company plans to develop a data search engine based on the data used by users. If the engine can provide users with search based on different criteria, its design will be more interactive. In this kind of testability design, which is open to users, people can gain a direct understanding of the data product system through their own manipulation and enhance the interaction between the individual and the digital environment.

5.4 Virtuality

In the computer field, virtuality is usually regarded as the opposite of "physical" or "real". But the indicators mentioned here are developed from Deleuze's philosophical concept and are almost equated with possibility or potential.

Uncertainty is necessary for human self-realization or creation. As Deleuze said, if all the uncertainty in the world is cleared and everything is decided, how can we imagine creation? [28] Potentiality means that people cannot pre-define self-existence or ability, but always move towards identity or personality development that has never existed before [29]. It can be seen that virtuality is a necessary condition for the development of human environmental competence.

The use of data by enterprises in the way of intelligent algorithms will pose a threat to the virtuality as a constitutive element of human life. Intelligent algorithm analysis, which is cherished by market subjects, can obtain the probability of people's behavior tendency through complex data mining and accurate dynamic modeling. The wide impact of this technology makes the whole world and human behavior predictable. Through prediction, the algorithm denies the possibility of human existence of the environment [30]. Through induction and control, companies regulate people's remaining possibilities. This erosion of virtuality will lead to the inhibition of human environmental competence.

Therefore, the degree of containment of virtuality should become an important indicator of moral criticism and evaluation of data use plans. In order to obtain positive evaluation, it is necessary to adjust the design of intelligent algorithm. For example, some scholars propose to introduce the concept of capability into risk assessment so that the latter is no longer dominated by the calculation of re-sources or utility, but also covers the possibility of weakening capacity [31]. This provides a new dimension for judging the acceptability of risk. This kind of virtual-oriented scheme can provide standard guidance for the technical design of data use.

5.5 Participable

In the broadest sense, participable refers to the possibility that the subject can influence a particular social or technological process through his or her own judgment or action. In a sense, the meaningful data that emerge at the micro level of concrete operation, related to human intention, can avoid the simplification of facts and the solidification of thinking caused by classification logic. When developing digital products and services, if enterprises take into account more knowledge and judgments derived from people's daily experience, they can reduce the negative impact of computer classification logic on human environmental ability by importing situational facts.

The import of situational facts can first of all be realized by the participable of the developers of data products or services. The new generation of artificial intelligence technology is moving towards this kind of participable, paying attention not only to the computational trend of problem solving in algorithms and related disciplines, but also to the way of solving problems under the condition of man-machine cooperation. Guide computer thinking from model abstraction and logical reasoning ability to knowledge transfer and comprehensive evaluation ability [32].

In addition, the participation of users or consumers can bring together the experience of a wider range of stakeholders and promote participation to a new level between subjects. For example, when some clothing enterprises use data to make optimization decisions, they not only collect consumer transaction data and market data, but also incorporate consumer opinions and suggestions on clothing size, color, fabric and style into decision analysis [33] as separate data types to balance the abstractness of the algorithm model and data increase.

Another typical example of opening up to users is online crowdsourcing, which is a community cooperation model that breaks the boundaries of data technology and capital specificity and explores individual potential initiative and creativity [34]. This model can absorb the micro-creativity and micro-content of different users (to meet the diversified spiritual needs) into the development process of data products and services and form an open data value production network. Therefore, the principle of moral criticism also encourages and supports this kind of participatory design in the process of data utilization.

6 Conclusions and Future Work

Theorists' mistrust of new technology is responsible for social prospects and the human situation. The huge value created by data use and the accompanying moral crisis make the digital economy like a driverless G-Series High-Speed Train. If we revel in the benefits brought by new technologies and ignore the hidden and far-reaching harm to human development, it will push human and social values into great risks.

In order to avoid the most universal threat of data use in the context of computer, public sectors and enterprises must avoid weakening or damaging the environmental conpetence of other individuals, organizations and groups, or inhibiting the development of their environmental competence. In order to avoid the most general threat to data use in this computerized background, public sectors and enterprises must avoid weakening or damaging the environmental competence of other individuals, organizations and groups, or inhibiting the development of it. This is the most general principle of moral criticism in the digital age.

With reference to this principle, we regard society as a mutually beneficial cooperation for the common goal of developing the broadest range of environmental competence. In order to fully realize the requirements of this principle, any society as a whole should be encouraged to develop the broadest range of environmental competence, while individuals must be guaranteed equal rights to develop the widest range of environmental competence within their own endowments, and the environmental competence actually developed by each person need to be compatible with others. Finally, through the evaluation indicators like cognitive interest, technological size, interactivity, virtuality and participable, regulators can implement this moral principle in a specific context, combined with the technical design and planning of data use.

The analysis of this paper is only the initial achievement of this research. Issues like the improvement of the evaluation indicators; the specific way of the moral principle being incorporated into the legal system, and the specific system to support effective operation of this principle, need further study to deal with.

This paper is the research result of the National Social Science Foundation project "Research on legal Governance system and Legislative change in Digital Society" (20&ZD178).

References

1. Deakin, S., Markou, S.: Is Law Computable? Critical Perspectives on Law and Artificial Intelligence. Hart Publishing, Oxford (2020)
2. Li, S.Q.: Research on the legalization of data science and technology ethics. J. Chin. Juris. **2022**(04), 114–134 (2022). https://doi.org/10.14111/j.cnki.zgfx.20220721.007
3. Cybersecurity Law of the People's Republic of China: Article 28
4. Fjeld, J., Achten, N., Hilligoss, H., Nagy, A., Srikumar, M.: Principled artificial intelligence: mapping consensus in ethical and rights-based approaches to principles for AI. Berkman Klein Center Research Publication No. 2020-1, p. 5. https://ssrn.com/abstract=3518482 or https://doi.org/10.2139/ssrn.3518482
5. Zhu, T.Y.: The distinction between ethics and morality—some thoughts on rewriting Chinese ethics. J. East China Norm. Univ. Philos. Soc. Sci. Ed. **50**(01), 1–8 + 177 (2018). https://doi.org/10.16382/j.cnki.1000-5579.2018.01.001
6. Kant, I.: Critique of Practical Reason, 2nd edn. Cambridge University Press, Cambridge (2015)
7. Kant, I.: Groundwork of the Metaphysics of Morals, 2nd edn. Cambridge University Press, Cambridge (2012)
8. Rawls, J.: A Theory of Justice, 2nd edn. Belknap Press, An Imprint of Harvard University Press (1999)
9. Flikschuh, K.: Kant's kingdom of ends: metaphysical, not political. J. World Philos. (2015)
10. Oakeshott, M.: Experience and its Modes, Reissue Cambridge University Press, Cambridge (2015)
11. Packard, V.: The Naked Society. Penguin Books, Harmondsworth (1971)
12. Berry, D.: Critical Theory and the Digital, 1st edn, Bloomsbury Academic (2014)
13. Steele, F.: Physical Settings and Organization Development, 1st edn, Addison Wesley Publishing Company (1973)

14. The French Data Protection Authority (CNIL) (2019): How can humans keep the upper hand? The ethical matters raised by algorithms and artificial intelligence
15. Department of Industry Innovation and Science: Australia's artificial intelligence ethics framework (2019). https://www.industry.gov.au/data-and-publications/australias-artificial-intellige nce-ethics-framework/australias-ai-ethics-principles
16. The High-Level Expert Group on AI: Ethics guidelines for trustworthy AI. https://digital-str ategy.ec.europa.eu/en/library/ethics-guidelines-trustworthy-ai
17. French National Information and Freedom Commission, European data Protection Commissioner, Italian personal data Protection Commissioner: Declaration ethics and data protection in artificial intelligence. J. Off. Informatization (2019)
18. Chen, L.: Labor order under "Digital Control". J. Sociol. Res. (2020)
19. Zhang, J.J., Lin, Y.: A study on Carl Otto Appel's theory of cognitive purport. J. Theor. Trends Abroad (2009)
20. Habermas, J.: Knowledge and Human Interests, 2nd edition. Beacon Press (1972)
21. In April 2014, Wei Zexi, a sophomore at Xi'an University of Science and Technology, was diagnosed with synovial sarcoma. According to the recommendation of Baidu search engine, he went to Beijing second Hospital of the Armed Police to receive biological immunotherapy. It is reported that this therapy is a foreign clinical obsolete technology. Wei family hollowed out his savings and finally failed to achieve the therapeutic effect. Wei Zexi posted a post in February 2006 (two months before his death) questioning that the medical information in Baidu's bidding rankings misled consumers and led to delays in treatment
22. Guidelines for the classification and classification of Internet platforms (draft for soliciting opinions). https://finance.sina.com.cn/jjxw/2021-10-29/doc-iktzscyy2531191.shtml
23. Guide to the implementation of subject responsibility on Internet platforms (draft for soliciting opinion). https://www.cqn.com.cn/zj/content/2021-10/29/content_8747098.htm
24. According to section 1714.43 (a) (1) of the California supply chain Transparency Act, the Act is aimed at "retail and manufacturing operators with annual global earnings of more than $100 million". The $25 million under the California Consumer Privacy Act is most likely to refer to revenue derived locally in California, excluding global revenue outside California
25. 2018 California Code Civil Code – Civ Division 3 – Obligations Part 4 -1.81.5 - California Consumer Privacy Act of 2018 Section 1798.140(a) (b)
26. Deng, S.L.: Research progress of interaction in information. J. Books Inf. (2008)
27. Garousi, V., Federer, M., Kılıçaslan, F.: A survey on software testability. J. Inf. Softw. Technol. **108**, 35–64 (2018)
28. Deleuze, G.: Bergsonism. Zone Books, New York (1988)
29. Rouvroy, A.: Technology, virtuality and Utopia: governmentality in an age of autonomic computing. In: Law, Human Agency and Autonomic Computing: The Philosophy of Law Meets the Philosophy of Technology, pp. 119–140. Routledge (2011)
30. Costa, L.: Virtuality and capabilities in a world of ambient intelligence. Springer, Namur, Belgium (2016). https://doi.org/10.1007/978-3-319-39198-4
31. Murphy, C., Gardoni, P.: Design, risk and capabilities. In: Oosterlaken, I., van den Hoven, J. (eds) The Capability Approach, Technology and Design. Philosophy of Engineering and Technology, vol. 5, pp. 173–188. Springer, Dordrecht (2012). https://doi.org/10.1007/978-94-007-3879-9_10
32. Chen, Z., Liu, N.Y., Yin, Y.Q., Liu, C.C., Wang, Y.M.: From algorithm to participation in building computational models: concept evolution and capability structure of computational thinking in the perspective of human-machine coordinated. J. Distance Educ. **39**(04), 34–41 (2021). https://doi.org/10.15881/j.cnki.cn33-1304/g4

33. Xiao, J.H., Wu, Y., Liu, Y., Xie, K.: New product development innovation with customer digitalized engagement: a comparative case study from the Firrn-customer coevolutionary perspective. J. Manage. World. https://doi.org/10.19744/j.cnki.11-1235/f.2018.08.013
34. Shu, W., Jin, C., Liang, L.: Analysis of collaborative and self-organizing innovation effect of the network crowdsourcing model. J. Sci. Res. Manage. **35**(4), 26 (2014). https://doi.org/10.19571/j.cnki.1000-2995.2014.04.004

ELECTRA-KG: A Transformer-Knowledge Graph Recommender System

Benjamin Kwapong[1], Amartya Sen[2], and Kenneth K. Fletcher[1(✉)] [ID]

[1] University of Massachusetts Boston, Boston, MA 02125, USA
{benjamin.kwapong001,kenneth.fletcher}@umb.edu
[2] Oakland University, Rochester, MI 48309, USA
sen@oakland.edu

Abstract. Knowledge graphs (KGs) are becoming popular in recommender systems in recent times because of the wealth of side information they provide. Many researchers rely on KGs to help resolve the issues of cold start, diversity, and explainability in recommendations. However, the existing approaches usually ignore entity descriptions, which are essential in providing content information for entities in KGs. In this work, we propose a contextual language model for KG completion known as ELECTRA-KG (Efficiently Learning an Encoder that Classifies Token Replacements Accurately). We formulate the recommendation task as a KG link prediction task where we have an incomplete knowledge graph and we use state-of-the-art approaches to complete it. We do this by identifying missing facts among entities from our test data. To evaluate and validate our method, we perform a couple of experiments. First, we run experiments to demonstrate how well our model compares to state-of-the-art KG embedding models. Second, we run further experiments with our model on the tag recommendation task and compare our results to existing baselines. Our results show that our model outperforms the existing baselines on the tag recommendation task.

Keywords: Reinforcement learning · word2vec · Recommender systems · Language modeling · Deep learning

1 Introduction

Recommender systems (RS) have been developed at different levels with different approaches to help resolve the challenge of choice-making due to the abundance and variety of information. The aim, however, remains the same - to dynamically serve customized content to users based on their profiles [12,13], preferences [9,20,21], or expected needs [10]. Despite many advances in RS, they still suffer from data sparsity limitation, and it is sometimes challenging to explain their results [11]. To resolve the data sparsity limitation and improve explainability in RS, researchers use side information (such as social media, etc.)

W. Qingyang and L.-J. Zhang (Eds.): SCC 2022, LNCS 13738, pp. 56–70, 2022.
https://doi.org/10.1007/978-3-031-23515-3_5

to augment their training data. Among all the side information for RS, knowledge graphs (KGs) have shown to be very valuable. This is because they allow for hybrid graph-based recommendation methods comprising both collaborative and content information [19]. They play vital roles in many applications for instance, question answering [8], word embedding [36], browsing knowledge and data visualization [16]. Using KG as side information can find latent connections and improve precision, extend user interest reasonably and bring explainability in recommendations [32].

Expanding existing KGs requires scalability in the existing inference approaches. Recent embedding methods such as [14,22,35] have mainly focused on capturing the structure of the KG into some latent space for easy and efficient manipulation. They, do not factor in the semantics of the facts that the KG triples convey, which is vital for a recommendation because items and their attributes can be mapped into the KG to reveal the mutual relations between items [39]. They typically learn the same textual representations of entities and relations such that for a word w, there is a fixed vector representation anywhere it occurs in the corpus (i.e., either an entity or a relation). The problem here is that, words in entity and relation descriptions can have different meanings or importance weights in different triples. For example, consider these three sentences:

1. *My dog **runs** around the house every day,*
2. *She **runs** a very successful business,* and
3. *The computer program **runs** at the beginning of each month.*

The first sentence refers to the dog moving quickly with the legs, the second refers to managing a business, and the last sentence refers to a machine working. All three sentences use the relation ***runs***, but it means something different in each of the three sentences. This means that using a fixed vector representation for a word irrespective of where it appears is not accurate. Therefore, to ensure relations between users, items, and users' preferences are captured accurately, users and their side information can also be integrated into the KG [41].

Recent advances in natural language processing (NLP) and natual language understanding (NLU) have produced state-of-the-art models such as BERT [7], XLNet [37], RoBERTa [23] and ELECTRA [5] which can learn contextualized word embeddings with large amount of free text. The performance of XLNet is comparable to that of RoBERTa, while RoBERTa (and XLNet) outperform BERT on all General Language Understanding Evaluation (GLUE) tasks. ELECTRA on the other hand performs comparably to RoBERTa and XLNet while using less than 25% of the compute. In this paper, we propose the ELECTRA-KG RS, which models a specific relation in a KG as the recommendation link and thereby turns KG completion into a sequence classification problem.

The main contributions of this paper are summarized as follows:

1. We fine-tune a transformer pre-trained model (ELECTRA) to embed our KG into vector representations. We introduce the ELECTRA-KG (Efficiently

Learning an Encoder that Classifies Token Replacements Accurately Knowledge Graph), which utilizes a custom KG built with the triples in our datasets as textual sequences.

2. We provide preliminary studies conducted on four benchmark datasets to establish that our model outperforms most of several state-of-the-art models in terms of accuracy, Mean rank, and Hit Rate.

3. We model a specific relation as the recommendation link and turn KG completion into a sequence classification problem, where we compute a scoring function of the triples that can help to determine the plausibility of a triple or a relation from our fine-tuned model.

4. We conduct extensive experiments on our proposed method and compare our results to nine relevant baselines. Our results show that our proposed model generally outperforms all the baselines.

2   Background and Preliminary Work

2.1   Efficiently Learning an Encoder that Classifies Token Replacements Accurately (ELECTRA)

ELECTRA [5] is a new pre-training approach that trains two neural networks (Transformers), a generator G and a discriminator D. Each one primarily consists of an encoder (e.g., a Transformer network) that maps a sequence on input tokens $x = [x_1, ..., x_n]$ into a sequence of contextualized vector representations $h(x) = [h_1, ..., h_n]$. For a given position t (i.e. $x_t = [MASK]$), the generator outputs a probability for generating a particular token x_t and the discriminator predicts whether the token x_t is "real", i.e., that it comes from the data rather than the generator distribution (Fig. 1).

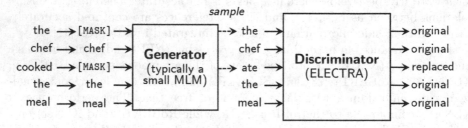

Fig. 1. An overview of replaced token detection. The generator can be any model that produces an output distribution over tokens, but in this case, a small masked language model is used, that is trained jointly with the discriminator. Although the models are structured like in a GAN, the generator is trained with maximum likelihood rather than adversarially due to the difficulty of applying GANs to text. After pre-training, the generator is thrown out and only the discriminator (the ELECTRA model) is fine-tuned on downstream tasks [5].

The generator is trained to perform masked language modeling (MLM). Given an input $x = [x_1, x_2, ..., x_n]$, MLM first select a random set of positions (integers between 1 and n) to mask out $m = [m_1, ..., m_k]$. The tokens in the selected positions are replaced with a $[MASK]$ token: denoted as $x^{masked} = \text{REPLACE}(x, m, [MASK])$. The generator then learns to predict the original identities of the masked-out tokens. The discriminator is trained to distinguish tokens in the data from tokens that have been replaced by generator samples. More specifically, a corrupted example $x^{corrupt}$ is created by replacing the masked-out tokens with generator samples and training the discriminator to predict which tokens in $x^{corrupt}$ match the original input x. After pre-training, the generator is thrown out and the discriminator is fine-tuned on downstream tasks.

Inspired by KG-BERT [38], we fine-tune the ELECTRA pre-trained model for knowledge graph completion (see Fig. 2). We ran experiments based on four widely used datasets (WN11 [30], FB13 [30], WN18RR [6], and FB15K-237 [6]) and compared our initial results to several state-of-the-art baselines (including KG-BERT) in order to establish the effectiveness of our ELECTRA-KG before modifying it for our recommendation task.

We conduct two main preliminary experiments with our ELECTRA-KG model. First, is the triple classification, which aims to judge whether a given triple (h, r, t) is correct or not. Second, is the link (entity) prediction task that predicts the head entity h given $(?, r, t)$ or predicts the tail entity t given $(h, r, ?)$ where ? means the missing element. Our model performs best for the triple classification task, with an average accuracy of 92%. For link prediction task, our model outperforms the other baseline models in terms of mean rank (MR) and performs averagely in terms of Hits@10 for the two datasets used. Through this empirical study, we extended the ELECTRA-KG model for RS in this work.

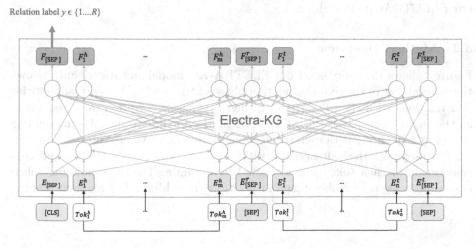

Fig. 2. The ELECTRA-KG model inspired by KG-BERT [38]

3   ELECTRA-KG RS

3.1   Problem Definition

Let $S = \{s_1, s_2, ..., s_m\}$ be the set of services in a service repository such that each service, s, is described by a tuple:

$$s < N, D_S, T, D_T, G, D_G, A >$$

where N is the service name, D_S is the service description document, T is the set of tags, D_T is the set of tag descriptions, G is the set of genres, D_G is the set of genre descriptions, and A is also a tuple of other auxiliary attributes, such as the set of categories that the service belongs to.

Let $S^N = \{s_1^N, s_2^N, ..., s_m^N\}$ be the set of services names, $S^{D_S} = \{s_1^{D_S}, s_2^{D_S}, ..., s_m^{D_S}\}$ be the set of services description documents, $S^T = \{s_1^T, s_2^T, ..., s_m^T\}$ be the set of tags, $S^{D_T} = \{s_1^{D_T}, s_2^{D_T}, ..., s_m^{D_T}\}$ be the set of tag descriptions, $S^G = \{s_1^G, s_2^G, ..., s_m^G\}$ be the set of genres, $S^{D_G} = \{s_1^{D_G}, s_2^{D_G}, ..., s_m^{D_G}\}$ be the set of genre descriptions, and $S^A = \{s_1^A, s_2^A, ..., s_m^A\}$ be the set of auxiliary attributes for all services in the service repository, such that each service S_i has a name S_i^N, a description document $S_i^{D_S}$, tags S_i^T, tag descriptions $S_i^{D_T}$, genres S_i^G, genre descriptions $S_i^{D_G}$, and auxiliary attributes S_i^A.

Service KG Generation. Given S^N, S^T, S^G, and S^A, we construct a knowledge graph **G**, such that:

$$\mathbf{G} = \{(h, r, t) \mid h, t \in \mathbf{E}, r \in \mathbf{R}\} \tag{1}$$

where h and t are the head and tail entities respectively and r is the relation that links them, $\mathbf{E} = \{S^N \cup S^T \cup S^G \cup S^A\}$ is the set of entities and $\mathbf{R}$ is the set of relations that exists between the entities. The KG, **G**, will serve as input to our ELECTRA-KG model.

3.2   Method Overview

Figure 3 shows the overview of our ELCTRA-KG model and Algorithm 1 shows the general flow of the recommendation phase of the model. We represent entities and relations with their descriptions, then take the description word sequences as the input sentence of the ELECTRA model for fine-tuning. We model our triples as sequences, with each triple being a sequence. We use the special token [SEP] to separate the sentences of entities and relations (triples). The input representation of each token is constructed by summing the corresponding token embedding, segment embedding and position embedding. The segment embed-

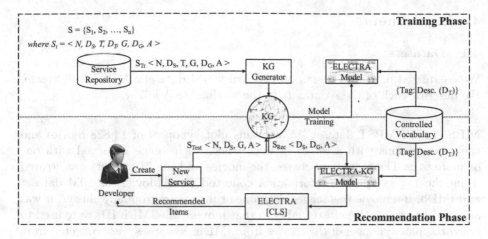

Fig. 3. Overview of the proposed ELECTRA-KG recommendation model.

ding keeps alternating between 0 and 1. Thus the tokens in sentences of the head and tail entities share the same segment embedding, and the relation has a different embedding. We then feed the token representations into the ELECTRA model (Sect. 2.1). We model a specific relation in our KG as the recommendation link such that if we want to recommend an item, we just have to determine what the tail entity will be at the end of that link/relation. To make a recommendation for a user, we make the user the head entity, and the recommendation link the relation. We then test each of the items in our controlled vocabulary as the tail entity and select the highest scoring triple.

Algorithm 1. ELECTRA-KG Recommendation

1: **procedure** ELECTRA-KG($\{cntrl\_vocab : descriptions\}$):
2:      $recommendation\_dict \leftarrow defaultdict(list)$
3:      **for** $head\ and\ relation\ in\ test\_data$ **do**:
4:          $cntrl\_vocab\_dict \leftarrow defaultdict()$
5:          **for** $tail\ in\ cntrl\_vocab$ **do**:
6:              $triple \leftarrow head - relation - tail$
7:              $vocab\_score \leftarrow Score(triple)$
8:              $cntrl\_vocab\_dict[tail] = vocab\_score$
9:          **end for**
10:          $Sort\ cntrl\_vocab\_dict\ by\ vocab\_score$
11:          $recommendation\_dict = cntrl\_vocab\_dict.keys()[: k]$
12:      **end for**
13:      **return** $recommendation\_dict$
14: **end procedure**

---

4   Experiments

4.1   Datasets

We conducted our experiments on two real world datasets: MPST and Steam. We describe each of these datasets in the sections that follow.

MPST. The MPST dataset [15] contains plot synopses of 14,828 movies and their associations with a set of 71 tags; where each movie is tagged with one or more tags. The mapping between the movies and the 71 clusters was created using the tag assignment information collected from MovieLens 20M dataset and IMDb. If a movie was tagged with one or more tags from any cluster, it was assigned the respective cluster label to that movie. The IMDb IDs were used to crawl the plot synopses of the movies from IMDb. Synopses were collected from Wikipedia for the movies without plot synopses in IMDb or if the synopses in Wikipedia were longer than the synopses in IMDb. These steps resulted in the MPST corpus that contains 14,828 movie plot synopses where each movie has one or more tags. The lowest number of tags per movie is 1 and the highest number of tags per movie is 25. For the purpose of our experiments, we cross-referenced the movies in the MPST dataset with the movies from the popular Movielens 20M dataset in order to obtain genre information for the movies.

Steam. The steam dataset provides information about various aspects of games gathered from the Steam Store and SteamSpy APIs, such as its name, genres, categories, tags, and description.

4.2   Metrics

The following metrics were used in this experiment:

Recall @ K: is the fraction of tags among the real tag set for a mashup that are recommended. It is defined as:

$$Recall@K = \frac{|tags_{rec} \cap tags_{actual}|}{|tags_{actual}|}$$

where $tags_{rec}$ is the recommended tag set, and $tags_{actual}$ is the actual tag set for the mashup.

Precision @ K: is the fraction of recommended tags that are among the real tag set for a mashup. It is defined as:

$$Precision@K = \frac{|tags_{rec} \cap tags_{actual}|}{|tags_{rec}|}$$

Where $tags_{rec}$ is the recommended tag set, and $tags_{actual}$ is the actual tag set for the mashup.

F-Measure @ K: is a measure of the recommendation accuracy. It is the weighted harmonic mean of the precision and recall given as:

$$F - Measure@K = 2 * \frac{Precision * Recall}{Precision + Recall}$$

4.3 Baselines

We compare the recommendation results from our ELECTRA-KG Model with the following baselines with respect to Precision, Recall and F-Measure.

– **Logistic Regression:** Logistic regression is a statistical model that in its basic form uses a logistic function to model a binary dependent variable. More complex extensions exist that cater for more complex cases. Mathematically, a binary logistic model has a dependent variable with two possible values, such as pass/fail which is represented by an indicator variable, where the two values are labeled "0" and "1".
– **Random Forrest:** Random forests are an ensemble learning method for classification, regression and other tasks that operates by constructing a multitude of decision trees at training time and outputting the class that is the mode of the classes (classification) or mean/average prediction (regression) of the individual trees.
– **XGBoost** [4]: XGBoost (eXtreme Gradient Boosting) is an optimized distributed gradient boosting library designed to be highly efficient, flexible and portable. It implements machine learning algorithms under the Gradient Boosting framework. XGBoost provides a parallel tree boosting that solves many data science problems in a fast and accurate way.
– **Multinomial Naive Bayes (MNB)** [17]: MNB implements the naive Bayes algorithm for multinomially distributed data, and is one of the two classic naive Bayes variants used in text classification (where the data are typically represented as word vector counts, although tf-idf vectors are also known to work well in practice). It is suitable for classification with discrete features (e.g., word counts for text classification).
– **Complement Naive Bayes (CNB)** [29]: CNB is an adaptation of the standard multinomial naive Bayes (MNB) algorithm that is particularly suited for imbalanced data sets. Specifically, CNB uses statistics from the complement of each class to compute the model's weights. The inventors of CNB show empirically that the parameter estimates for CNB are more stable than those for MNB. Further, CNB regularly outperforms MNB on text classification tasks.
– **Multi-Label kNN (MLkNN)** [40]: MLkNN uses k-Nearest Neighbors find nearest examples to a test class and uses Bayesian inference to select assigned labels.

4.4 Results and Discussion

The following experiments were conducted and the results have been presented alongside the baselines in Table 1.

Table 1. A comparison of Recommendation Accuracy (Precision, Recall, F-Measure) for the MPST and Steam Datasets. Numbers in boldface are the best performing in their column, while the underlined numbers are the second best.

Dataset	MPST			Steam		
Model	Precision	Recall	F1	Precision	Recall	F1
Logistic Regression	0.3869	0.4339	0.4091	0.4468	0.6747	0.5376
Random Forrest	**0.6385**	0.1194	0.2012	**0.7388**	0.3692	0.4924
XGBoost	0.5959	0.1998	0.2993	0.7196	0.4686	0.5676
MNB	0.2544	0.3504	0.2948	0.7253	0.3162	0.4404
CNB	0.3623	0.3985	0.3795	0.7041	0.3340	0.4531
MLkNN	0.3087	0.1234	0.1763	0.6521	0.4152	0.5074
Cosine_Sim-KG	0.5409	0.6608	0.5949	0.6505	0.6766	0.6633
Jaccard_Sim-KG	0.5524	0.6756	0.6078	0.6672	0.6937	0.6802
ELECTRA-KG	0.5649	**0.6887**	**0.6209**	0.6721	**0.6993**	**0.6854**

- **Cosine_Sim-KG:** We use node cosine similarity [1,18] to find the most similar entities and then recommend appropriate tags. In the context of a KG, the cosine similarity $\sigma_{i,j}$ of nodes i and j is the cosine of the angle between vectors A_i and A_j:

$$\sigma_{i,j} = \frac{\sum_k A_{i,k} A_{j,k}}{\sqrt{\sum_k A_{i,k}^2} \sqrt{\sum_k A_{j,k}^2}} \quad (2)$$

where, A_i and A_j refers to the vector representations of the entities at nodes i and j respectively with dimension k. We build the vector of each node by assigning 1 to where there is a presence of another node in it's adjacency list, and 0 otherwise. So we have that:

$$\sigma_{i,j} = \frac{n_{i,j}}{\sqrt{d_i d_j}} \quad (3)$$

where $n_{i,j}$ is the number of neighbors shared by nodes i and j, d_i is the degree of node i and d_j is the degree of node j. That is, cosine similarity between i and j is the number of neighbors shared by i and j divided by the geometric mean of their degrees.

In cases where the recommended tags are not enough, we use tag augmentation to support.

- **Jaccard_Sim-KG:** We use node jaccard similarity [1] to find the most similar entities and then recommend appropriate tags. Given two nodes, i and j, the Jaccard Similarity $\mathcal{J}_{ij}$ between i and j is the number of neighbors shared by i and j divided by the number of items in the union of the neighbors if i and j (i.e. the number of unique elements between i and j). That is:

$$\mathcal{J}_{ij} = \frac{n_{i,j}}{d_i + d_j - n_{i,j}} \quad (4)$$

where $n_{i,j}$ is the number of neighbors shared by nodes i and j, d_i and d_j are the degree of nodes i and j respectively.

In cases where the recommended tags are not enough, we use tag augmentation to support.
- **ELECTRA-KG:** We build our KG with the triples in our datasets as textual sequences. By modeling a specific relation as the recommendation link, we turn KG completion into a sequence classification problem. Once entity and relation representations have been learned before hand, we can compute the score of any triple as long as $h, t \in \mathbb{E}$ and $r \in \mathbb{R}$. By doing so, we can determine the plausibility of a triple or a relation from our fine-tuned model.

A comparison of the results from our experiments and the baselines have been populated in Table 1. The best performance is in bold and the second best is underlined. Since the F1 tells the overall accuracy, we use it as the basis for our comparison. Details of the comparison are listed below:

For the MPST Dataset, our ELECTRA-KG model outperformed the other baselines as follows: 51.8% better than Logistic Regression, 208.6% better than Random Forest, 107.5% better than XGBoost, 110.6% better than MNB, 63.6% better than CNB, and 252.2% better than MLkNN. For the other models described in the paper, ELECTRA-KG was 4.4% better than Cos_Sim-KG and 2.2% better than Jaccard_Sim-KG.

For the Steam Dataset, our ELECTRA-KG model outperformed the other baselines as follows: 27.5% better than Logistic Regression, 39.1% better than Random Forest, 20.8% better than XGBoost, 55.6% better than MNB, 51.3% better than CNB, and 35.1% better than MLkNN. For the other models described in the paper, ELECTRA-KG was 3.3% better than Cos_Sim-KG and 0.8% better than Jaccard_Sim-KG.

In general, even though some of the baselines performed well on Precision and others performed well on recall, our model outperformed them all in terms of the F1 score. The models which outperformed our model on precision performed abysmally on recall, and those that outperformed our model on recall performed abysmally on precision.

5   Related Work

5.1   Knowledge Graph for Recommendation:

Researchers in recent times have successfully used knowledge graphs at various levels to build recommender systems. In [27], they build a knowledge graph of user-item and item-item relations, then use a neural network to learn property specific vector representations of users and items. These representations are used to create property-specific user-item relatedness features, which are in turn fed into learning to rank algorithms to learn a global relatedness model that optimizes top-N item recommendations. In [32], they propagate user preferences over the set of knowledge entities by automatically and iteratively extending a user's potential interests along links in the knowledge graph. The multiple "ripples" activated by a user's historically clicked items are thus superposed to form the preference distribution of the user with respect to a candidate item, which could be used for predicting the final clicking probability. The authors in [34] generate path representations by composing the semantics of both entities and relations. By leveraging the sequential dependencies within a path, they allow effective reasoning on paths to infer the underlying rationale of a user-item interaction. Furthermore, they design a new weighted pooling operation to discriminate the strengths of different paths in connecting a user with an item, endowing their model with a certain level of explainability. KGs have also been used to assist in the sharing of latent features and the learning of high-order interactions between items/entities in recommender systems [33].

Knowledge Graph completion helps to add new triples to a KG due to the incomplete nature of KGs. To do this efficiently, embedding methods have been developed to capture the inherent structure of KGs. The main KG applications are: Triple Classification, Link prediction, Entity Resolution and Entity Classification. Triple Classification [14,35] aims to judge whether a given triple (h, r, t) is correct or not, e.g., $(Boston, LocatedIn, Massachusetts)$ should be classified as a true fact while $(Bronx, LocatedIn, Massachusetts)$ should be classified as false. Once entity and relation representations have been learned before hand, we can compute the score of any triple as long as $h, t \in \mathbb{E}$ and $r \in \mathbb{R}$. The link prediction task [14,35] predicts the head entity h given $(?, r, t)$ or predicts the tail entity t given $(h, r, ?)$ where ? means the missing element. Entity Resolution/Alignment [2,25] consists of verifying whether two entities refer to the same object, while Entity Classification [25,26] aims to categorize entities into different semantic categories.

5.2 Language Modeling

Building large-scale labeled datasets is very expensive due to annotation costs, and hence it poses a great challenge for most Natural Language Processing (NLP) tasks. The abundance of large-scaled unlabeled corpora means that the ability to learn a good representation of such corpora will help in transfer learning tasks. Significant performance gains on many NLP tasks have been reported in recent studies. These gains are mainly due to the help of representation extracted from the pre-trained language models. Traditional language models such as Word2Vec [24] and Glove [28] used feature-based approaches to learn context-independent words vectors. More recent approaches like GPT [3], BERT [7], RoBERTa [23] use pre-trained models for NLP transfer learning tasks such as question answering, next sentence prediction. These pre-trained models capture rich semantic patterns from free text. In the context of KGs, models such as the ones proposed by [31] learn contextual embeddings on entity-relation chains (sentences) generated from random walks in a KG, then use the embeddings as initialization of KG embeddings models like TransE. Others like [42] and [38] use GPT or BERT to generate tail tokens, enhance language representation or classify triples. Unlike these studies which do not tackle recommendations, in order to recommend items from our model, we use descriptions of entities and relations as input and fine-tune ELECTRA to compute plausibility scores of triples generated from a specific recommendation relation.

6 Conclusion

In this paper, we have showed how effective the ELECTRA language model can be for embedding knowledge graphs. Specifically, we compared and reported the performance of ELECTRA-KG with several state-of-the-art models on four benchmark datasets. We went ahead to tune our ELECTRA-KG for tag recommendation using 2 real world dataset. Our results showed that our model significantly outperformed well known baselines. For future work, we plan to pre-train our ELECTRA from scratch to determine the effect of the pre-training data on our recommendation task.

References

1. Amer, A.A., Abdalla, H.I., Nguyen, L.: Enhancing recommendation systems performance using highly-effective similarity measures. Knowl.-Based Syst. **217**, 106842 (2021). https://doi.org/10.1016/j.knosys.2021.106842, https://www.sciencedirect.com/science/article/pii/S0950705121001052
2. Bordes, A., Glorot, X., Weston, J., Bengio, Y.: A semantic matching energy function for learning with multi-relational data. Mach. Learn. **94**(2), 233–259 (2013). https://doi.org/10.1007/s10994-013-5363-6
3. Brown, T.B., et al.: Language models are few-shot learners. CoRR abs/2005.14165 (2020). https://arxiv.org/abs/2005.14165
4. Chen, T., Guestrin, C.: XGBoost: a scalable tree boosting system. In: Proceedings of the 22nd ACM SIGKDD International Conference on Knowledge Discovery and Data Mining, pp. 785–794 (2016)
5. Clark, K., Luong, M., Le, Q.V., Manning, C.D.: ELECTRA: pre-training text encoders as discriminators rather than generators. CoRR abs/2003.10555 (2020). https://arxiv.org/abs/2003.10555
6. Dettmers, T., Minervini, P., Stenetorp, P., Riedel, S.: Convolutional 2D knowledge graph embeddings. In: Proceedings of the Thirty-Second AAAI Conference on Artificial Intelligence and Thirtieth Innovative Applications of Artificial Intelligence Conference and Eighth AAAI Symposium on Educational Advances in Artificial Intelligence. AAAI 2018/IAAI 2018/EAAI 2018. AAAI Press (2018)
7. Devlin, J., Chang, M.W., Lee, K., Toutanova, K.: BERT: pre-training of deep bidirectional transformers for language understanding. In: Proceedings of the 2019 Conference of the North American Chapter of the Association for Computational Linguistics: Human Language Technologies, Volume 1 (Long and Short Papers), pp. 4171–4186. Association for Computational Linguistics, Minneapolis (2019). https://doi.org/10.18653/v1/N19-1423, https://aclanthology.org/N19-1423
8. Dong, L., Wei, F., Zhou, M., Xu, K.: Question answering over freebase with multi-column convolutional neural networks. In: Proceedings of the 53rd Annual Meeting of the Association for Computational Linguistics and the 7th International Joint Conference on Natural Language Processing (Volume 1: Long Papers), pp. 260–269. Association for Computational Linguistics (2015). https://doi.org/10.3115/v1/P15-1026
9. Fletcher, K.K., Liu, X.F.: A collaborative filtering method for personalized preference-based service recommendation. In: 2015 IEEE International Conference on Web Services, pp. 400–407 (2015). https://doi.org/10.1109/ICWS.2015.60

10. Fletcher, K.: Regularizing matrix factorization with implicit user preference embeddings for web API recommendation. In: 2019 IEEE International Conference on Services Computing (SCC), pp. 1–8. IEEE (2019)
11. Fletcher, K.K.: A method for dealing with data sparsity and cold-start limitations in service recommendation using personalized preferences. In: 2017 IEEE International Conference on Cognitive Computing (ICCC), pp. 72–79. IEEE (2017)
12. Fletcher, K.K.: A quality-based web API selection for mashup development using affinity propagation. In: Ferreira, J.E., Spanoudakis, G., Ma, Y., Zhang, L.-J. (eds.) SCC 2018. LNCS, vol. 10969, pp. 153–165. Springer, Cham (2018). https://doi.org/10.1007/978-3-319-94376-3_10
13. Fletcher, K.K.: A quality-aware web API recommender system for mashup development. In: Ferreira, J.E., Musaev, A., Zhang, L.-J. (eds.) SCC 2019. LNCS, vol. 11515, pp. 1–15. Springer, Cham (2019). https://doi.org/10.1007/978-3-030-23554-3_1
14. Ji, G., He, S., Xu, L., Liu, K., Zhao, J.: Knowledge graph embedding via dynamic mapping matrix. In: Proceedings of the 53rd Annual Meeting of the Association for Computational Linguistics and the 7th International Joint Conference on Natural Language Processing (Volume 1: Long Papers), pp. 687–696. Association for Computational Linguistics, Beijing (2015). https://doi.org/10.3115/v1/P15-1067, https://aclanthology.org/P15-1067
15. Kar, S., Maharjan, S., López-Monroy, A.P., Solorio, T.: MPST: a corpus of movie plot synopses with tags. In: et al. (eds.) Proceedings of the Eleventh International Conference on Language Resources and Evaluation (LREC 2018). European Language Resources Association (ELRA), Paris (2018)
16. Kertkeidkachorn, N., Ichise, R.: T2KG: an end-to-end system for creating knowledge graph from unstructured text. In: AAAI Workshops (2017)
17. Kibriya, A.M., Frank, E., Pfahringer, B., Holmes, G.: Multinomial naive bayes for text categorization revisited. In: Webb, G.I., Yu, X. (eds.) AI 2004. LNCS (LNAI), vol. 3339, pp. 488–499. Springer, Heidelberg (2004). https://doi.org/10.1007/978-3-540-30549-1_43 .
18. Kwapong, B., Anarfi, R., Fletcher, K.K.: A knowledge graph approach to mashup tag recommendation. In: 2020 IEEE International Conference on Services Computing (SCC), pp. 92–99 (2020). https://doi.org/10.1109/SCC49832.2020.00021
19. Kwapong, B., Fletcher, K.: A knowledge graph based framework for web API recommendation. In: 2019 IEEE World Congress on Services (SERVICES), vol. 2642–939X, pp. 115–120 (2019). https://doi.org/10.1109/SERVICES.2019.00039
20. Kwapong, B.A., Anarfi, R., Fletcher, K.K.: Personalized service recommendation based on user dynamic preferences. In: Ferreira, J.E., Musaev, A., Zhang, L.-J. (eds.) SCC 2019. LNCS, vol. 11515, pp. 77–91. Springer, Cham (2019). https://doi.org/10.1007/978-3-030-23554-3_6
21. Kwapong, B.A., Anarfi, R., Fletcher, K.K.: Collaborative learning using LSTM-RNN for personalized recommendation. In: Wang, Q., Xia, Y., Seshadri, S., Zhang, L.-J. (eds.) SCC 2020. LNCS, vol. 12409, pp. 35–49. Springer, Cham (2020). https://doi.org/10.1007/978-3-030-59592-0_3
22. Lin, Y., Liu, Z., Sun, M., Liu, Y., Zhu, X.: Learning entity and relation embeddings for knowledge graph completion. In: Proceedings of the AAAI Conference on Artificial Intelligence, vol. 29, no. 1 (2015). https://ojs.aaai.org/index.php/AAAI/article/view/9491
23. Liu, Y., et al.: Roberta: A robustly optimized BERT pretraining approach. CoRR abs/1907.11692 (2019). http://arxiv.org/abs/1907.11692

24. Mikolov, T., Sutskever, I., Chen, K., Corrado, G., Dean, J.: Distributed representations of words and phrases and their compositionality. In: Proceedings of the 26th International Conference on Neural Information Processing Systems, NIPS 2013, vol. 2, pp. 3111–3119. Curran Associates Inc., USA (2013)
25. Nickel, M., Tresp, V., Kriegel, H.P.: A three-way model for collective learning on multi-relational data. In: Proceedings of the 28th International Conference on International Conference on Machine Learning, ICML 2011, pp. 809–816. Omnipress, Madison (2011)
26. Nickel, M., Tresp, V., Kriegel, H.P.: Factorizing yago: scalable machine learning for linked data. In: Proceedings of the 21st International Conference on World Wide Web, WWW 2012, pp. 271–280. Association for Computing Machinery, New York (2012). https://doi.org/10.1145/2187836.2187874, https://doi-org.ezproxy.lib.umb.edu/10.1145/2187836.2187874
27. Palumbo, E., Rizzo, G., Troncy, R.: Entity2rec: learning user-item relatedness from knowledge graphs for top-n item recommendation. In: Proceedings of the Eleventh ACM Conference on Recommender Systems, RecSys 2017, pp. 32–36. Association for Computing Machinery, New York (2017). https://doi.org/10.1145/3109859.3109889, https://doi-org.ezproxy.lib.umb.edu/10.1145/3109859.3109889
28. Pennington, J., Socher, R., Manning, C.: GloVe: global vectors for word representation. In: Proceedings of the 2014 Conference on Empirical Methods in Natural Language Processing (EMNLP), pp. 1532–1543. Association for Computational Linguistics, Doha (2014). https://doi.org/10.3115/v1/D14-1162, https://aclanthology.org/D14-1162
29. Rennie, J.D., Shih, L., Teevan, J., Karger, D.R.: Tackling the poor assumptions of naive bayes text classifiers. In: Proceedings of the 20th International Conference on Machine Learning (ICML-2003), pp. 616–623 (2003)
30. Socher, R., Chen, D., Manning, C.D., Ng, A.Y.: Reasoning with neural tensor networks for knowledge base completion. In: Proceedings of the 26th International Conference on Neural Information Processing Systems, NIPS 2013, vol. 1, pp. 926–934. Curran Associates Inc., Red Hook (2013)
31. Wang, H., Kulkarni, V., Wang, W.Y.: Dolores: deep contextualized knowledge graph embeddings. ArXiv abs/1811.00147 (2020)
32. Wang, H., et al.: RippleNet: propagating user preferences on the knowledge graph for recommender systems. In: Proceedings of the 27th ACM International Conference on Information and Knowledge Management, CIKM 2018, pp. 417–426. ACM, New York (2018). https://doi.org/10.1145/3269206.3271739
33. Wang, X., Wu, H., Hsu, C.: Mashup-oriented API recommendation via random walk on knowledge graph. IEEE Access 7, 7651–7662 (2019). https://doi.org/10.1109/ACCESS.2018.2890156
34. Wang, X., Wang, D., Xu, C., He, X., Cao, Y., Chua, T.: Explainable reasoning over knowledge graphs for recommendation. CoRR abs/1811.04540 (2018). http://arxiv.org/abs/1811.04540
35. Wang, Z., Zhang, J., Feng, J., Chen, Z.: Knowledge graph embedding by translating on hyperplanes. In: Proceedings of the AAAI Conference on Artificial Intelligence, vol. 28, no. 1 (2014). https://ojs.aaai.org/index.php/AAAI/article/view/8870
36. Xu, C., et al.: RC-net: a general framework for incorporating knowledge into word representations. In: Proceedings of the 23rd ACM International Conference on Conference on Information and Knowledge Management, CIKM 2014, pp. 1219–1228. ACM, New York (2014). https://doi.org/10.1145/2661829.2662038

37. Yang, Z., Dai, Z., Yang, Y., Carbonell, J., Salakhutdinov, R.R., Le, Q.V.: XLNet: generalized autoregressive pretraining for language understanding. In: Wallach, H., Larochelle, H., Beygelzimer, A., d' Alché-Buc, F., Fox, E., Garnett, R. (eds.) Advances in Neural Information Processing Systems, vol. 32. Curran Associates, Inc. (2019). https://proceedings.neurips.cc/paper/2019/file/dc6a7e655d7e5840e66733e9ee67cc69-Paper.pdf

38. Yao, L., Mao, C., Luo, Y.: KG-BERT: BERT for knowledge graph completion. CoRR abs/1909.03193 (2019). http://arxiv.org/abs/1909.03193

39. Zhang, F., Yuan, N.J., Lian, D., Xie, X., Ma, W.Y.: Collaborative knowledge base embedding for recommender systems. In: Proceedings of the 22nd ACM SIGKDD International Conference on Knowledge Discovery and Data Mining, KDD 2016, pp. 353–362. Association for Computing Machinery, New York (2016). https://doi.org/10.1145/2939672.2939673, https://doi-org.ezproxy.lib.umb.edu/10.1145/2939672.2939673

40. Zhang, M.L., Zhou, Z.H.: ML-KNN: a lazy learning approach to multi-label learning. Pattern Recogn. **40**(7), 2038–2048 (2007)

41. Zhang, Y., Ai, Q., Chen, X., Wang, P.: Learning over knowledge-base embeddings for recommendation. ArXiv abs/1803.06540 (2018)

42. Zhang, Z., Han, X., Liu, Z., Jiang, X., Sun, M., Liu, Q.: ERNIE: enhanced language representation with informative entities. In: ACL (2019)

Neighbor Collaboration-Based Secure Federated QoS Prediction for Smart Home Services

Zhuo Xu, Jian Lin, Weiwei She, Jianlong Xu[✉], Zhi Xiong, and Hao Cai

College of Engineering, Shantou University, Shantou 515063, China
{20zxu3,20jlin3,17wwshe,xujianlong,zxiong,haocai}@stu.edu.cn

Abstract. Smart homes IoT (SHIoT) deploys various devices that can achieve rich functionality by invoking cloud services for better in-home experiences. Recommending the quality services will allow the devices to provide greater comfort to the homeowner. Traditional service recommendation methods require collecting the quality of service (QoS) data to achieve better recommendations but also pose privacy problems. Inspired by federated learning (FL), some privacy-preserving federated recommendation methods have been proposed. However, studies have demonstrated that user preferences and even raw data can be inferred in FL. To implement service recommendations in SHIoT while protecting the edge privacy, we propose a secure federated QoS prediction method with neighbor collaboration (NCSF). By collaboration, users in NCSF upload perturbed updates, while the perturbations are offset during server aggregation without affecting the global model. Experiments on real-world datasets show that NCSF can achieve same recommendation quality and stronger privacy protection as the FL approach of plaintext aggregation.

Keywords: Smart home IoT · QoS prediction · Cloud service · Federated learning

1 Introduction

The Internet of Things (IoT) connects the physical world to the cyber world through networks built by connecting billions of objects [1]. Benefiting from IoT technology, smart home systems also constantly improve the convenience and comfort of people's lives. With the development of communication technologies and edge computing, more and more devices are being added to the smart home IoT (SHIoT) [2]. These devices are often at the edge of the SHIoT network and are limited by computing resources and storage capacity [3].

Based on the service-oriented architecture (SOA), edge devices enrich the functionality of the smart home by combining different services to build new applications [4]. The everything-as-a-service (XaaS) paradigm has given rise to a large number of mobile services with similar or identical functions developed by different service providers [5]. Selecting the quality service among these mobile services with similar functionality has become imperative. For home users, it is

W. Qingyang and L.-J. Zhang (Eds.): SCC 2022, LNCS 13738, pp. 71–85, 2022.
https://doi.org/10.1007/978-3-031-23515-3_6

almost impossible to invoke all possible services to record all values and then select the best one. To cope with such a dilemma, the QoS-based service selection approach is proposed. Due to the sparsity of services being invoked, how to predict QoS accurately becomes a prerequisite for service recommendation.

Conventional QoS-based service selection methods rely on cloud computing platforms with powerful computing and storage resources, which require users in the network to upload local data for building rich information to train the learning model. But data transmission is bandwidth intensive and the synchronization of data collection is difficult to guarantee due to the variability of users' network environments. Moreover, laws and regulations such as General Data Protection Regulation (GDPR) restrict the transmission of private data [6]. This is because of the risk of data leakage in sending sensitive data to the cloud. With no guarantee of privacy and security, users are less likely to agree to upload private data. To simultaneously ensure user privacy and get better learning results, Google has proposed a distributed learning technique called Federated Learning (FL) [7]. In the FL architecture, private data are stored locally and participate in the training of the model, and the update of weights is left to the parameter server for aggregation and allocation.

However, if the security of the transmission and aggregation cannot be ensured, the uploaded information is still at risk of being leaked in FL. In QoS prediction, user's privacy mainly contains identity privacy, value privacy, and model privacy. Identity privacy contains users' private information, such as geographic location, physiological characteristics, etc. Value privacy is the QoS observed by the user. Model privacy is the trained model used to predict QoS. In federated matrix factorization (FMF), the federated version of matrix factorization, users share the same latent feature space and it is easy to get the user's invocation records of the services from the uploaded gradients [8]. FMF uses the aggregation method of FedAvg [9] to collect the weights of all users, which may lead to the leakage of user preferences. Moreover, it has also been demonstrated that an untrusted central server is able to recover privileged information about an individual user's private training data through gradient inference attacks [10].

To ensure the accuracy of the prediction, while being able to protect the privacy of users. We propose a secure federated QoS prediction method based on neighbor cooperation. This is a lightweight and scalable federated learning approach that implements FL through edge servers in collaboration with a central server. With the help of neighbors, edge family users use pairwise noise to scramble the weighted data, making it impossible for malicious entities to easily obtain private information. In summary, our contributions are as follows:

1) We propose a privacy-preserving method for edge users based on neighborhood cooperation for user QoS prediction. User privacy protection is achieved with smaller communication cost and computational cost.
2) We propose a privacy-enhancing approach based on mask and data slicing that improves the difficulty for malicious entities to obtain user privacy and prove that our approach is simple but effective.

3) We investigate the effectiveness of our method on a real-world dataset and compare it with FedAvg aggregation to verify its recommendation quality. We analyze the impact of different parameter settings on the model and provide possible explanations. We also experimentally discuss the impact of user dropout on the proposed approach.

2 Related Work

The purpose of service recommendation and selection is to provide higher quality services to users. Quality of Service (QoS) is the non-functional attribute of services, which is also defined as the user experience attribute. Common QoS include throughput, response time, availability, etc. The key to implementing service recommendation and selection in mobile and IoT environments is to predict the QoS values of candidate services from the observed QoS records. As a popular method in recommender systems, collaborative filtering (CF) is also widely applied in QoS prediction [11–13]. Recently some researchers have noticed the potential privacy threats in QoS prediction and proposed many QoS prediction methods for privacy protection. For example, differential privacy (DEDP) methods that obfuscate the original QoS data [4], QoS prediction methods based on homomorphic encryption [14], etc.

The proposal of federated learning provides a new idea for privacy protection. Only parameters are exchanged between the two types of entities in FL instead of the transmission of raw data, which can achieve privacy-preserving purposes in the ideal case. Zhang et al. [15] then proposed a federated matrix factorization method (EFMF) for QoS prediction, which also improves model efficiency by reducing system overhead. However, some studies have shown that the federated matrix factorization that only transmits latent factors also has the risk of privacy leakage [8]. The work of [10] demonstrates that malicious users can even infer the original data. Therefore, a more secure FL model needs to be designed to resist smarter privacy thieves.

Chai et al. [16] use homomorphic encryption to protect the privacy of FL participants, but homomorphic encryption introduces a non-negligible computational overhead. Perifanis et al. proposed a federated version of NCF, FedNCF [17]. They used a privacy-preserving aggregation method based on Secure Multiparty Computation (SMC). Xu et al. [18]noticed the possible Freerider attack in FL and proposed a global model assignment scheme based on reputation and contribution. Liu et al. [19] designed a scalable privacy-preserving aggregation scheme for the user dropout problem, which can tolerate participants to drop out at any time. Their approach relies on the additive homomorphism property of the Shamir secret sharing scheme.

3 Method

3.1 Problem Definition

We consider a Federated SHIoT with multiple home users as shown in Fig. 1, where each home contains several devices that need to invoke web services. This

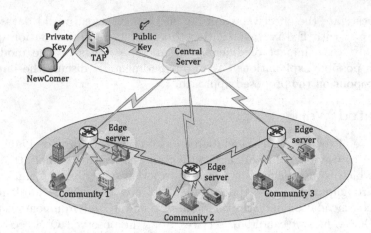

Fig. 1. Overall network architecture for federated edge computing.

network has some subnets, each of which represents a community network. The edge users of each subnet are managed by community edge servers, and all edge servers are connected to a central server. To facilitate data richness, edge users are unitized into households, each of which has a gateway (housekeeper) with communication and computing capabilities. The network topology of devices inside the home is invisible to outsiders, and requests for services are sent outward by the housekeeper. Note that the entities of this network can communicate with each other, all users want to build a federated QoS prediction framework that guarantees privacy. We assume that both the user and the server are are honest but curious, but they do not collude. That is, the threat to the security of the system comes from the inference of independent entities on the weight.

Definition 1. Given N participants and M services, where each participant represents an edge house, $P = \{U_i, S_j, q_{ij}\}$, where $U = \{1, ..., i, ..., N\}$ is the user ID, $S = \{1, ..., j, ..., M\}$ is the service ID, and $q_{ij} \in Q$ denotes the observed QoS value of user U_i for service S_j. QoS-based service selection aims to predict the unknown QoS from the recorded $\{U, S, q\}$.

3.2   Federated QoS Prediction

Local Training: In the federated framework, each user U_i keeps a record of the invoked services $\{U_i, S, q_{ij}\}$. U_i train the local model with its data to get the weights W_i. Two QoS prediction methods are performed locally, one is the classical matrix factorization [15] and the other is the neural network-based QoS prediction [20]. Note that in our proposed approach, the same prediction method is used locally by users during a complete learning cycle.

Multi-level Servers: The edge server is used to aggregate the global learning parameters within this community and control the learning progress of the community users. The central server, for its part, maintains global parameters across multiple communities and controls the global learning process. The servers at each level have two functional modules: a task generator ,and an aggregator. The task generator is used to generate task descriptions, including the IDs of users participating in the current round of learning that need to be updated locally, the public key, and the global parameters generated by the aggregator (which are randomly initialized in the first round). The aggregator performs the collection and averaging of the local updates for each user to form the new global parameters.

Trusted Authorized Party (TAP): In addition, NCSF introduce a Trusted Authorized Party (TAP) for new user registration and authorization. The main function of TAP is to assign a unique index (ID), the public key, and the private key when a new user joins the system.

3.3   Privacy Protection via Neighbor Collaboration

The Secret of Pairing Sharing: The privacy issue that needs to be addressed is to make the server agnostic to the weight updates of individual users. The FedAvg is vulnerable to attacks by HBC servers, and the insecure transmission channel increases the risk of privacy leakage as participants transmit the computation results in plaintext. A reasonable way to implement privacy-preserving aggregation is to use an effective secure aggregation scheme such as SecAvg [21]. SecAvg enables the coordination server to compute the update sum without revealing the weights generated by each participant.

Consider a set of clients c participating in FL, $i, j \in c, i \neq j$, where each participant is paired with others and agrees on a random seed. Noises are added according to the following rules:

$$\hat{W}_i = \begin{cases} W_i + \sum_{i,j \in c} N_{ij} & i < j \\ W_i - \sum_{i,j \in c} N_{ji} & i > j \,, \end{cases} \quad (1)$$

where $\hat{W}_i$ is the uploaded weight from client i, N_{ij} and N_{ji} denote the noises generated by client i and client j using the agreed random seeds.

At aggregation, the sum of the updates from all users W_g^{sum} is calculated in accordance with Eq. (2).

$$\begin{aligned} W_g^{sum} &= \sum_{i \in c} \hat{W}_i \\ &= \sum_{i \in c} W_i + \sum_{i,j \in c} N_{ij} - \sum_{i,j \in c} N_{ji} \\ &= \sum_{i \in c} W_i. \end{aligned} \quad (2)$$

Under such a rule, to obtain the weight of a client requires knowing its random seed agreed with other participants or the noise generated accordingly. In addition, if a client drops out, then all clients paired with it need to discard the seeds they agreed with. This all increases the cost of communication.

The idea of neighbor-based collaboration is that neighbors keep a secret of each other for perturbing weights and edge devices upload the perturbed weights to protect privacy. Unlike the SecAvg described above, a client participating in FL communicates with only a few neighbors, reducing the communication cost. A simplest idea is that a client i is paired with only one neighbor j. Then the weight of the resulting obfuscation is:

$$\hat{W}_i = W_i + N_{ij}, \qquad \hat{W}_j = W_j - N_{ji}. \tag{3}$$

$$\begin{aligned} \hat{W}_i + \hat{W}_j &= W_i + N_{ij} + W_j - N_{ji} \\ &= W_i + W_j. \end{aligned} \tag{4}$$

However, since the assignment of client pairs is done by the HBC server, according to such a rule the server is able to get the sum of weights of clients i, j. If we consider i and j as a new user, then there is also the risk of its privacy leakage.

Privacy Enhanced with Masks: To address the pairwise privacy leakage from single-neighbor collaboration, we use masks to enhance user privacy, which is a lightweight and scalable multi-neighbor collaboration aggregation approach.

Specifically, we consider a subnetwork scenario with no less than three edge devices participating. The participants are $\{a, b, c\}$ each of which is paired with and only with two neighbors, so the obtained user pairs are (a, b), (b, c), and (c, a), with each client pair agreeing on a random seed. When client a gets the local weight W_a, two randomly generated masks with the same shape as W_a and corresponding bits summing to 1 are generated. Multiplying W_a with the corresponding bits of the two masks respectively, the weights W_{a1} and W_{a2} of client a's slice are obtained. Then add the noises N_{ab} and N_{ac} which are agreed with the two neighbors to the weights of the two slices respectively to get the two weights $\hat{W}_{ab}$ and $\hat{W}_{ac}$ that a actually upload. Similarly, we can obtain $\hat{W}_{ba}, \hat{W}_{bc}, \hat{W}_{ca}, \hat{W}_{cb}$.

In general, for the weight $hatW_{ik}$ uploaded by user i and the $hatW_{ik}$ it produces by adding noise N_{ij} to the slice weight W_{ik}, the sum of the update weights is calculated as:

$$\begin{aligned} W_g^{sum} &= \sum_{i \in c, k=1,2} \hat{W}_{ik} \\ &= \sum_{i \in c, k=1,2} W_{ik} + \sum_{i \in c, j \in n, i>j} N_{ij} - \sum_{i \in c, j \in n, i<j} N_{ji} \\ &= \sum_{i \in c} W_i, \end{aligned} \tag{5}$$

3.4   Handling Dropout Users

As mentioned above, the noise used to perturb the user's local updates is generated using pairs of random seeds that are agreed with their neighbors. If a user drops out, then the noise in the updates uploaded by its neighbors cannot be offset. We simply handle user dropouts. If the weight of the user's corresponding neighbor is not received when aggregating weights by the server, it should inform the user and re-pair the users to achieve the collection of the remaining weights.

3.5 Algorithm Descriptions

A complete update round is as follows: the central server generates the learning task and distributes the selected list of task participants and the global update parameters to each edge server. The edge server checks the list, extracts the user IDs of this community, randomly scrambles the order and then performs user pairing, and delivers the tasks to the users in the community in the form of (user1ID, user2ID, user2 public key, global weight W_g). After receiving its task, user1 performs the current round of local learning updates using W_g. While updating, user1 uses the received paired user IDs as well as the public key to communicate with paired user2 to negotiate a random seed. After negotiating the random seed and completing the local update user1 perturbs the local update W_i using the random noise generated by the random seed. Finally the scrambled update $\hat{W}_i$ is uploaded to the server located at the edge of the community. After receiving updates from all participants in this community, the edge server aggregates and sends the aggregated community updates to the central server using the same strategy of perturbation.

Edge Clients: Unlike the traditional federated learning, the edge users of NCSF need to negotiate random seeds with their users in addition to performing local updates. User i encrypts two seeds $E(seed_{ia})$ and $E(seed_{ib})$ using the public keys Pk_a and Pk_b from the received task description, and sends them to the corresponding neighbors. Similarly, i receives two seeds $E(seed_{ai})$ and $E(seed_{bi})$ encrypted with i's public key Pk_i from its neighbors a and b. i uses its own private key Sk_i to decrypt these two secret messages to obtain $seed_{ai}$ and $seed_{bi}$, which are combined with $seed_{ia}$ and $seed_{ib}$ sent out by itself to form the mutually agreed seeds $seed_a$, $seed_b$.

The user gets W_i after performing a traditional local update using the received global parameters W_g, and uses mask privacy enhancement to obtain W_{i1}, W_{i2} of the slices. Random noises are generated using the two seeds of the agreement to perturb the slices separately and finally generate W_{ia}, W_{ib}.

Edge Servers: The edge server takes on two responsibilities, one of which is to generate task descriptions for the community and distribute them to the edge users in the community. The other is to perform weight aggregation for the edge users in the community and upload it to the central server.

In the task description generation phase, the edge server first picks all the users in this community from the received set of users who need to perform the tasks in this round. Then it performs user pairing based on the set number of neighbors n. Take $n = 2$ as an example to pair user i with the two users a and b.

The edge server generates a task description of $\{i, (a, Pk_a), (b, Pk_b), W_g\}$, where i denotes the user who received the task and (a, Pk_a) is the ID of i's neighbor a and its public key, and W_g is the global weight. When performing weight aggregation for edge users, the edge server simply accumulates the updates uploaded by the edge users in the community and then uploads them to the central server.

Central Server: With the assistance of the edge server, the functions of the central server are simplified. The central server only needs to perform the assignment of global tasks, $|\mathcal{P}|$, and the aggregation of community updates to generate global weights. The central server receives the community updates W_e from the edge server aggregation, where e denotes the edge server. All W_e are summed and then averaged with $|\mathcal{P}|$ to obtain the global parameter W_g for the new round, $|\mathcal{P}|$ is the total number of users performing the task in this round. It should be noted that in case of user dropouts, the edge server should inform the central server and subtract the number of dropout users in the aggregation.

3.6   Communication Overhead and Security Analysis

We consider a SHIoT system with E edge servers managing N participants with the number of neighbors set to M and discuss the computational and communication overheads of each entity in this system.

Computation Overheads: Each user's computational cost mainly depends on (i) computing random perturbations $O(M)$ for M neighbors (ii) adding noise $O(M^2)$ after mask operations on local updates, with the number of masks equal to the number of neighbors. Therefore, the computational complexity of each user participating in FL is $O(M + M^2)$. The central server is computationally involved only in aggregating and averaging the updates uploaded by all users, and its computational expenditure is $O(NM)$.

Communication Overheads: Each home user needs to communicate with M neighbors to obtain random seeds and to send M scrambled local updates to the edge server, which brings a communication cost of $O(3M)$. The communication of the edge server consists of sending tasks to users in the community and sending aggregated community updates to the central server. Therefore, the total communication overhead of the edge server is $O(2N + NM + E)$. The central server needs to deliver learning tasks to the edge server and receive community updates, with a communication overhead of $O(2E)$ In general, the number of neighbors is set to a smaller constant ($M \geq 1$). In this way, both the computation overhead and the communication overhead can be reduced to $O(N)$. This shows that our proposed NCSF is a lightweight secure federated learning method.

Security Analysis: Consider a community with n users and the number of neighbors of NCSF is m. Suppose there is an internal malicious privacy thief who wants to obtain local updates of other users from an insecure channel to infer user privacy. A simple case is to obtain the updates of its neighbors. Then, what this thief is able to obtain is the encrypted part of the seed $seed_1$, masked with scrambled local updates $\hat{W}_i$. This user wants to get the local updates of user i, and he needs to obtain the random seeds that i agreed with other neighbors. Since the seed is protected by an asymmetric encryption method, its cracking is very difficult. So, when the number of neighbors is set to 2, it is able to resist malicious internal privacy thieves. And, as the number of neighbors increases, it becomes more difficult to steal local updates. The same applies to HBC servers.

4 Experiments

In this section, we conduct experiments to show our model performance. Different experiments are designed to answer the following research questions:

RQ 1 Does NCSF affect the quality of predictions compared to FedAvg?

RQ 2 How does the setting of the number of neighbors affect the computational overhead imposed by users in NCSF?

RQ 3 What is the effect of different percentages of user participation on NCSF performance?

RQ 4 How does user dropout affect the model prediction results?

4.1 Dataset and Evaluation Metrics

To validate the effectiveness of the proposed NCSF, we conduct experiments on a widely used real-world dataset, WSDream [22]. This dataset contains records of 5828 service invoked by 339 users and provides data on two QoS attributes, response time (RT) and throughput (TP).

The performance of the prediction results is generally evaluated by mean absolute error (MAE), root mean square error (RMSE), and mean absolute percentage error (MAPE), which are also widely used evaluation metrics in QoS prediction tasks. The three metrics are calculated as follows:

$$MAE = \frac{\sum_{i,j} |R_{i,j} - \hat{R}_{i,j}|}{N},$$ (6)

$$RMSE = \sqrt{\frac{1}{N} \sum_{i,j} (R_{i,j} - \hat{R}_{i,j})^2},$$ (7)

$$MAPE = \frac{1}{N} \sum_{i,j} \frac{|R_{i,j} - \hat{R}_{i,j}|}{R_{i,j}},$$ (8)

where $R_{i,j}$ is the observed QoS value of service j invoked by user i, $\hat{R}_{i,j}$ is the predicted QoS value, and N is the number of all predicted values.

4.2 Experimental Settings

The experiments are conducted according to the proposed framework. All experiments in this article are compiled and tested on Windows system (CPU: Inter(R) Core(TM) i7-9700K CPU @ 3.60 GHz; GPU: Inter(R) UHD Graphics 630). All codes are written using the syntax of Python 3.8.

To simulate the service invocation records of real scenarios, we sparse the dataset by retaining a certain percentage of QoS values randomly, and here we refer to the percentage as matrix density.

Table 1. Performance comparison on Response Time (RT) and Throughput (TP).

Methods	Response time			Throughput		
	Matrix density = 20%			Matrix density = 20%		
	MAE	RMSE	MAPE	MAE	RMSE	MAPE
UPCC	0.6253	1.3879	2.1364	18.9192	48.2894	3.7816
IPCC	0.6344	1.4735	2.1304	23.9823	54.8972	3.0843
PMF	0.4712	1.2124	1.1867	15.0549	43.6669	1.1436
FMF	0.4417	1.2075	1.1085	16.0427	48.5663	1.0883
NCSF-FMF	0.4416	1.2122	1.0722	16.0485	48.5910	1.0879
Diff.	**0.0001**	**−0.0047**	**0.0363**	**−0.0058**	**−0.0247**	**0.0004**
GMF	0.4161	1.2144	0.8772	16.6310	42.9834	1.6281
Fed-GMF	0.4164	1.2893	1.0260	17.7571	49.6526	2.3976
NCSF-GMF	0.4165	1.2893	1.0269	17.7471	49.5534	2.3825
Diff.	**−0.0001**	**0.0000**	**−0.0009**	**0.0100**	**0.0992**	**0.0151**
LDCF	0.3357	1.2201	0.4198	13.1279	43.3071	0.8444
Fed-LDCF	0.3655	1.2439	0.5098	13.7302	43.5411	0.7981
NCSF-LDCF	0.3659	1.2439	0.5178	13.7247	43.8618	0.7762
Diff.	**−0.0004**	**0.0000**	**−0.0080**	**0.0055**	**−0.3207**	**0.0219**

4.3 Prediction Performance Comparison (RQ 1)

To demonstrate the efficiency of our proposed NCSF, we compare with the following approaches: *UPCC* [23], *IPCC* [24], *PMF* [25], *FMF* [15], *GMF* [20], *LDCF* [26].

In addition, we implement federated versions of GMF and LDCF for privacy preservation and name them Fed-GMF and Fed-LDCF, respectively. Here, the FedAvg is used to aggregate the updates of local users. We apply the proposed neighbor collaboration-based secure federated learning framework to MF, GMF, and LDCF and add the prefix *NCSF* to the method names.

We conduct experiments at a QoS matrix density of 20%, and for the federated version of the methods user participation is set to 100%. The performance

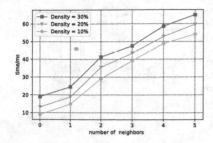

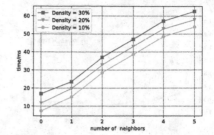

Fig. 2. Computation time per user for different neighbor settings on RT.

Fig. 3. Computation time per user for different neighbor settings on TP.

of the above methods on RT and TP is shown in Table 1, where smaller values represent better performance. $Diff.$ represents the difference of the metrics between the proposed NCSF and FedAvg, with positive indicating better performance and negative indicating worse performance.

As shown in Table 1, the neural network-based approach LDCF outperforms the other methods. Comparing the performance of the centralized prediction methods with the federated methods, it can be seen that the methods using federated learning lose some prediction accuracy while protecting privacy. The reduction in prediction accuracy is because both federated learning methods allocate the same global weights to each user, ignoring the variability among users. It can be seen from the difference between the evaluation metrics of FedAvg's aggregation method and NCSF's aggregation method that both perform almost the same. This indicates that our proposed method does not reduce the accuracy of federated prediction with further protection of user privacy.

4.4 Effect of the Number of Neighbors and Matrix Density (RQ 2)

The number of neighbors determines the number of updates uploaded by FL participants that are sliced. Security analysis tells us that the more neighbors there are, the more difficult it is for privacy thieves to access private data. But the overhead analysis also shows that the more neighbors bring more computation overhead and communication overhead as well. To explore the impact of increasing the number of neighbors, we conducted experiments using NCSF-LDCF as the prediction method. The number of neighbors is set to {0, 1, 2, 3, 4, 5}, and all other parameters are set the same. In addition, the abundance of data also affects the learning time of users. We conducted experiments on the computation time for a single user at matrix density settings of 10%, 20%, and 30%, respectively. The time of each user executing in each round is recorded and finally averaged. The results are shown in Figs. 2 and 3.

First, it can be seen that the computation time of a single user increases with the number of neighbors at the three matrix densities, which indicates that increasing the number of neighbors will bring computation overhead. At the same matrix density, the growth of computation time is close to linear. Secondly, the

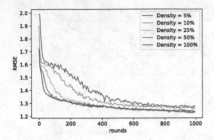
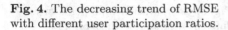
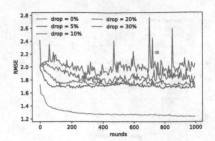

Fig. 4. The decreasing trend of RMSE with different user participation ratios.

Fig. 5. The result of different percentages of use's dropouts without handling.

higher the matrix density, the higher the computation time overhead. Since that the number of parameters of users increases with higher density.

4.5 Effect of the Participation Ratio (RQ 3)

As mentioned in Sect. 3, the central server selects users from the currently accessible group of users as learning takers when generating learning tasks. To study the effect of different proportions of participants on the training process, we set the density of users selected for each task round to {5%, 10%, 25%, 50%}. We conducted experiments using NCSF-LDCF as the prediction method.

It can be seen from Fig. 4 that the RMSE decreases rapidly in the first 25 rounds and slowly after 25 rounds for the five ratios set. The rate of RMSE decrease is different when different proportions of users participate in FL. Among them, the RMSE decreases most slowly when 5% of users perform FL, and the rate of decrease is the fastest when the participation ratio is 100%. This indicates that the larger the proportion of users, the faster the model converges. Moreover, the higher the user participation percentage, the smaller the RMSE value in the first round. The reason for this observation is that the higher the percentage of users, the richer the data available to the whole FL system. In addition, we can see that the trend of RMSE decrease at 50% user participation is very similar to that at 100% participation, which indicates that even if only half of the users participate in FL, a better learning efficiency can be achieved. This is due to the fact that although the proportion of users is fixed, the users are selected randomly each time, and multiple random selections can expand the coverage of user data and improve learning efficiency.

4.6 Effect of User Dropout (RQ 4)

We discuss the impact of user dropout in NCSF. Here, user dropout is defined as a user's exit after normal agreement seeding before uploading weights. That is, a dropped user is unable to upload updated weights, which causes part of the noise used by its neighbors not to be offset after aggregation, thus affecting global updates. We conducted experiments for this problem, in which the number of

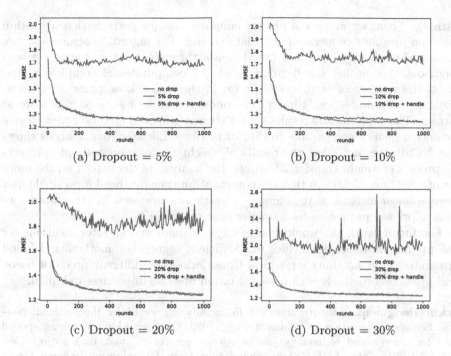

(a) Dropout = 5%   (b) Dropout = 10%

(c) Dropout = 20%   (d) Dropout = 30%

Fig. 6. Results of handling different percentages of use's dropouts.

users participating in each round of FL was 200, the number of neighbors is set to 2, and the percentage of dropped users is {0%, 5%, 10%, 20%, 30%}.

From Fig. 5, we can see that the dropped users have effects on our proposed neighbor collaboration-based federated learning. Besides, the more dropped users there are, the more the model convergence process is affected, and when the percentage of dropped users is 30%, the model even produces large fluctuations and fails to converge. And when the percentage of dropout users is 5%, the results of model convergence are significantly different from the experimental results of no user dropout. In Fig. 6, among all four proportions of dropped users, the RMSA of the dropped user handling strategy is very close to the result of no dropped users. This suggests that user dropouts should be considered in dynamic network environments.

5   Conclusion and Future Work

In this paper, we propose a secure federated learning framework based on neighbor collaboration, named NCSF, and apply this framework to the SHIoT to achieve privacy protection of edge home users while recommending services.

First, we design the edge federated learning framework containing two levels of servers, where the edge server is used for the management of community federated learning, and the central server unites multiple communities for federated learning. Then, we propose a privacy-enhanced weight perturbation algorithm based on neighbor cooperation and data slicing. The algorithm achieves secure transmission of weights in insecure channels through secret exchange between neighbors. And it has the flexibility and low computational complexity that allows the number of neighbors to be set in the task release phase for personalized privacy protection. Finally, we conducted experiments on a real-world dataset. The experimental results show that our proposed method can achieve a prediction quality comparable to that of FedAvg. Likewise, our analysis shows that NCSF does not affect the results of weight aggregation and only protects the process of weight transfer. Moreover, the analysis of the impact on the number of neighbors illustrates that the computation time overhead for a single user shows a linear increase as the number of neighbors increases. In other words, we achieve privacy protection by a smaller time overhead.

For future work, we would like to explore more and smarter solutions for QoS prediction. Examples include more efficient aggregation methods in FL and automated drop handling strategies. Considering the different needs of users, QoS prediction methods with personalization are also in our research plan.

Acknowledgment. This research was financially supported by the National Natural Science Foundation of China (No. 61702318), Guangdong province special fund for science and technology (major special projects + task list) project (No. STKJ2021201), 2020 Li Ka Shing Foundation Cross-Disciplinary Research Grant (No. 2020LKSFG08D), Guangdong Province Basic and Applied Basic Research Fund (2021A1515012527), Science and Technology Planning Project of Guangdong Province (2019B010116001), and Special projects in key fields of Guangdong universities (No. 2022ZDZX1008).

References

1. Koohang, A., Sargent, C.S., Nord, J.H., Paliszkiewicz, J.: Internet of things (IoT): from awareness to continued use. Int. J. Inf. Manage. **62**, 102442 (2022)
2. Yar, H., Imran, A.S., Khan, Z.A., Sajjad, M., Kastrati, Z.: Towards smart home automation using IoT-enabled edge-computing paradigm. Sensors **21**(14), 4932 (2021)
3. Chen, Y., Zhang, N., Zhang, Y., Chen, X., Wen, W., Shen, X.: Energy efficient dynamic offloading in mobile edge computing for internet of things. IEEE Trans. Cloud Comput. **9**(3), 1050–1060 (2019)
4. Zhang, Y., Pan, J., Qi, L., He, Q.: Privacy-preserving quality prediction for edge-based IoT services. Futur. Gener. Comput. Syst. **114**, 336–348 (2021)
5. Duan, Y., Fu, G., Zhou, N., Sun, X., Narendra, N.C., Hu, B.: Everything as a service (xaas) on the cloud: origins, current and future trends. In: 2015 IEEE 8th International Conference on Cloud Computing, pp. 621–628. IEEE (2015)
6. Yang, Q., Liu, Y., Chen, T., Tong, Y.: Federated machine learning: concept and applications. ACM Trans. Intell. Syst. Technol. (TIST) **10**(2), 1–19 (2019)
7. McMahan, B., Moore, E., Ramage, D., Hampson, S., Arcas, B.A.Y.: Communication-efficient learning of deep networks from decentralized data. In: Artificial Intelligence and Statistics, pp. 1273–1282. PMLR (2017)

8. Gao, D., Tan, B., Ju, C., Zheng, V.W., Yang, Q.: Privacy threats against federated matrix factorization. arXiv preprint arXiv:2007.01587 (2020)
9. Nilsson, A., Smith, S., Ulm, G., Gustavsson, E., Jirstrand, M.: A performance evaluation of federated learning algorithms. In: Proceedings of the Second Workshop on Distributed Infrastructures for Deep Learning, pp. 1–8 (2018)
10. Lam, M., Wei, G.-Y., Brooks, D., Reddi, V.J., Mitzenmacher, M.: Gradient disaggregation: breaking privacy in federated learning by reconstructing the user participant matrix. In: International Conference on Machine Learning, pp. 5959–5968. PMLR (2021)
11. Lei-lei Shi, L., Liu, L.J., Zhu, R., Panneerselvam, J.: QoS prediction for smart service management and recommendation based on the location of mobile users. Neurocomputing **471**, 12–20 (2022)
12. Xin, D., Jianlong, X., Cai, W., Zhu, C., Chen, Y.: OPRC: an online personalized reputation calculation model in service-oriented computing environments. IEEE Access **7**, 87760–87768 (2019)
13. Jianlong, X., et al.: NFMF: neural fusion matrix factorisation for QoS prediction in service selection. Connect. Sci. **33**(3), 753–768 (2021)
14. Badsha, S.: Privacy preserving location-aware personalized web service recommendations. IEEE Trans. Serv. Comput. **14**(3), 791–804 (2018)
15. Zhang, Y., Zhang, P., Luo, Y., Luo, J.: Efficient and privacy-preserving federated QoS prediction for cloud services. In: 2020 IEEE International Conference on Web Services (ICWS), pp. 549–553. IEEE (2020)
16. Chai, D., Wang, L., Chen, K., Yang, Q.: Secure federated matrix factorization. IEEE Intell. Syst. **36**(5), 11–20 (2020)
17. Perifanis, V., Efraimidis, P.S.: Federated neural collaborative filtering. Knowl.-Based Syst. **242**, 108441 (2022)
18. Xu, J., Xu, Z., Lin, J., She, W.: Double security guarantee: Protecting user privacy and model security in qos prediction. In: 2022 IEEE International Conference on Services Computing (SCC), pp. 140–145 (2022)
19. Liu, Z., Guo, J., Lam, K.-Y., Zhao, J.: Efficient dropout-resilient aggregation for privacy-preserving machine learning. IEEE Transactions Information Forensics and Security (2022)
20. He, X., Liao, L., Zhang, H., Nie, L., Hu, X., Chua, T.-S.: Neural collaborative filtering. In: Proceedings of the 26th International Conference on World Wide Web, pp. 173–182 (2017)
21. Pillutla, K., Kakade, S.M., Harchaoui, Z.: Robust aggregation for federated learning. arXiv preprint arXiv:1912.13445 (2019)
22. Zheng, Z., Zhang, Y., Lyu, M.R.: Distributed QoS evaluation for real-world web services. In: 2010 IEEE International Conference on Web Services, pp. 83–90. IEEE (2010)
23. Shao, L., Zhang, J., Wei, Y., Zhao, J., Xie, B., Mei, H.: Personalized QoS prediction forweb services via collaborative filtering. In: IEEE International Conference on Web Services (ICWS 2007), pp. 439–446. IEEE (2007)
24. Sarwar, B., Karypis, G., Konstan, J., Riedl, J.: Item-based collaborative filtering recommendation algorithms. In: Proceedings of the 10th International Conference on World Wide Web, pp. 285–295 (2001)
25. Mnih, A., Salakhutdinov, R.R.: Probabilistic matrix factorization. In: Advances in Neural Information Processing systems 20 (2007)
26. Zhang, Y., Yin, C., Qilin, W., He, Q., Zhu, H.: Location-aware deep collaborative filtering for service recommendation. IEEE Trans. Syst. Cybern. Syst. **51**(6), 3796–3807 (2019)

Research Directions in Process Modeling and Mining Using Knowledge Graphs and Machine Learning

John A. Miller and Rezwan Mahmud[✉]

School of Computing, University of Georgia, Athens, GA 30602, USA
jamill@uga.edu, rezwan.mahmud@uga.edu

Abstract. Services Computing has seen a dramatic rise in the last twenty years. The foundation for services provided by enterprises is business processes, so progress in the development of effective and efficient processes is of utmost importance. The design or modeling of business processes is a challenging task. Over the years many research and development efforts have paid dividends, including languages and notations like the Business Process Executing Language and the Business Process Modeling Notation, along with supporting methodologies and tools. Research in Semantic Web Services and Processes showed promise for the automation of services discovery and composition (orchestration/choreography). The current large-scale deployment of enterprise knowledge graphs by many organizations coupled with huge advancements in machine learning (particularly deep learning) provides new opportunities for advancing this automation forward.

Keywords: Business processes · Knowledge graphs · Machine-learning

1 Introduction

Many large organizations are developing enterprise knowledge graphs to organize their massive information infrastructure, that has potentially 10's of thousands products, billions of transactions, thousands of documents and Web pages, and thousands of processes. And this is just for the functional side of the business, e.g., not including HR or Financials. Typically, the enterprise knowledge graphs are based on a richer data model than the one for relational databases. Graph databases are emerging as the new standard, either of the Resource Description Framework (RDF) or Labeled Property Graph (LPG) form. With a rich schema level that, for example, is linked to one or more ontologies, these graph databases are often referred to as knowledge graphs.

Services computing has grown into a multi-billion dollar industry and has been used to improve the efficiency of internal business and outward-facing services (e.g., Business-to-Business (B2B) and Business-to-Consumer (B2C)). Behind most services are business processes. Due to the large number of processes and the requirement for agility, the need for technological innovation in process modeling continues.

W. Qingyang and L.-J. Zhang (Eds.): SCC 2022, LNCS 13738, pp. 86–100, 2022.
https://doi.org/10.1007/978-3-031-23515-3_7

This paper will examine how process modeling in the services era has progressed and examine the emerging approach of integrating process modeling with enterprise knowledge graphs. It will then consider how the use of temporal knowledge graphs can provide further innovations.

The paper is organized as follows: Sect. 2 discusses Knowledge Graphs, Enterprise Knowledge Graphs, and Temporal Knowledge Graphs. Progress in process modeling and mining is highlighted in Sect. 3. Section 4 explores how various types of knowledge graphs can be used with/for process modeling. The benefits that may accrue by utilizing machine learning are discussed in Sect. 5. Finally, Sect. 6 illustrates the advantages through a case study.

2 Knowledge Graphs

Although there are multiple definitions for Knowledge Graphs [14], if one starts with a Graph Database and elevates its semantic level, e.g., by adding some or all of the following, one may consider it a knowledge graph: hierarchical type system, constraints, and rules. There are two sets of software technologies that may be applied. One is from the Semantic Web Community and the other from the research and development of Graph Databases in the form of Labeled Property Graphs.

Work on Graph Databases started with the emergence of Database Systems as a field in the 1960s with the Network Data Model. Over the ensuing decades it lost out to its simpler cousin the Relational Data Model. How is it a cousin? At a high level, a Labeled Property Graph (LPG) may be defined as 4-tuple $G(V, E, \mathbf{p_v}, \mathbf{p_e})$ where

$$
\begin{aligned}
V &= \text{set of vertices} \\
E &= \text{set of edge} \\
p_v &= \text{function mapping vertices to their properties} \\
p_e &= \text{function mapping edges to their properties}
\end{aligned}
$$

Assuming one of the properties of a vertex specifies a type (e.g., Student or Course), vertices of the same type can be collected into a vertex-type, or table in the relational model. To handle the edges going between two vertex types, if the relationship is many-to-one, the edge attributes and an identifier for the target vertex may be added as properties/attributes on the many side. For the many-to-many case, an intermediate association table can be added.

Due to its simpler nature, the relational data model became the predominate data model during the decade of the 1970s. In the 1980s several data models and corresponding database systems were developed including Object-Oriented Databases, Deductive Databases, and Graph Databases. The new wave saw richer and higher level capabilities with the Graph Databases compared to the earlier Network Databases.

The 1990s, saw the emergence of the World Wide Web, which allowed the linkage of and search for documents on the Internet. The Web is a graph, so the 2000s ushered in two significant movements: the Semantic Web and NoSQL. The relational model broke up the graph (as discussed above) for the sake of simplicity, but with the Web pushing the linkage of Web pages or more generally resources, relational databases would not scale.

The NoSQL movement includes key-value stores, document databases, and graph databases (the movement is really an attempt to supplement relational database technology with other useful options). The strong need coupled with more capable computer technology, combined to accelerate NoSQL databases. Two present examples are MongoDB for storing documents and Neo4j as a graph database system.

On the Semantic Web side, the initial focus was linkage, making an HTML `href` more explicit and maintainable by utilizing Resource Description (RDF). An RDF store is a collection of triples of the form (subject, predicate, object). A triple is like an edge in an edge-labeled multi-graph. Built upon RDF were languages for schema and specifying ontologies, RDF Schema, and Web Ontology Language (OWL), respectively. In addition, languages for query formulation, constraints and rules have been developed, SPARQL, SHACL, and SWRL/RIF, respectively. These two movements were indirectly linked and given more momentum by Google in 2012 committing to the use of knowledge graphs.

2.1   Enterprise Knowledge Graph

Unlike large-scale comprehensive knowledge graphs like DBPedia or YAGO, an Enterprise Knowledge Graph (EKG) is focused on organizing an enterprise's information assets, although for companies like Google the scope is broad. Noy et al. [30] compare Knowledge Graphs from five large tech firms: Microsoft, Google, Facebook, eBay, and IBM. For example, Google added meta-types to its knowledge graph to support additional consistency checking. Facebook is challenged with dealing with conflicting information from different sources. They utilize providence information and create confidence levels for assertions.

Graph Databases allow optional schema, however, due to the need to anchor an enterprise's information in meaningful ways, EKGs should have schemas. The purpose of the schema is to capture the structure and processes of an organization. The concepts should be well defined and related to each other by concept inclusion or connections via roles/properties. As such one way to design an EKG schema is to start with an accepted ontology and extend or adapt it. Doing so will benefit interoperability between enterprises as needs arise.

After the initial EKG schema is built, the population of EKG begins, e.g., using Labeled Property Graphs or RDF-triple stores. Knowledge Graphs are flexible and the schema may grow as needed. Both the schema and data store are graphs where new vertices and edges may be added, as well as links between the schema and data store (or between the T-Box and A-Box in Semantic Web terminology). Population involves extracting information from relational databases, data warehouses, data lakes, corporate documents, and Web pages/documents.

Some massive and detailed data may be simply referenced or summarized in the EKG (many organizations have a huge number of relational tables each with many attributes having names that are hard for those not in the group actively using the table to understand). The EKG should serve the enterprise as a whole.

Building and maintaining a knowledge graph that continually extracts information from multiple sources is difficult, especially for maintaining high-quality [33]. To have a good organizational structure and enhanced interoperability standards should be used as a foundation. Standard ontologies or high-level schema are available at `schema.org`. In [33], they provide a strategy for extracting relevant parts of `schema.org` and adding customizations.

2.2 Temporal Knowledge Graphs

The modern world is being constantly monitored either by saving actions done by users (e.g., in event logs) or sensors collecting data. The effect is two-fold: The amount of data expands rapidly (big data), and the need to make time a central player in the storage and analysis of data substantially increases.

A Temporal Knowledge Graph (TKG) adds timestamps to vertices and edges, allowing the changes to the graph to be recorded over time. Extending the LPG based definition, a TKG may be defined as a 6-tuple $G(V, E, \mathbf{p_v}, \mathbf{p_e}, t_v, t_e)$ where the first four elements are the same as defined before and the last two are timestamps on vertices and edges, respectively. Alternatively, one may extend RDF triples into quads $= \{(s, p, o, t)\}$, where s is a subject, p is a predicate, o is an object, and t is a timestamp. Adding time allows the dynamics of a system or organization to be studied or analyzed. Missing values may be imputed and future values may be forecasted.

3 Process Modeling and Mining

A process (e.g., Business Process, Web Service Composition, or Workflow) has a collection of dependent actions (or activities) that occur over time. The dependencies may be depicted in a graph, e.g., action a_i must come before action a_j, as an edge $a_i \rightarrow a_j$. Many graph and graph-like diagrammatic structures have been proposed over the years and have led to the present Business Process Modeling Notation (BPMN) standard.

As mentioned EKGs maintain widely usable information about the corporation and IT processes. Both EKGs and process models are critical to the survival of the organization. Furthermore, processes disconnected from corporate information are less helpful, as additional effort is required to apply, maintain, upgrade and understand the processes within the organization.

3.1   Business Process Modeling Notation

There have been many forms of modeling notations, formalisms, diagrams, and languages developed for modeling processes and workflows. This section will limit the discussion of the services era that began at the start of the millennium.

Some notable languages [17,24] include, Yet Another Workflow Language (YAWL) [41], Event-Driven Process Chains (EPC) [26], and Business Process Execution Language (BPEL) [5] as well as those developed for Semantic Web Services, e,g., OWL for Services (OWL-S), Web Service Modeling Ontology (WSMO), Web Service Definition Language for Services (WSDL-S), and Semantic Annotations for WSDL (SASWDL). Process modeling languages have been classified into those that are graph-based and those that are rule-based [17,24]. Focusing on graph-based languages, the vertices represent basic steps (actions/activities), while the edges represent dependencies, either control or data. Although some languages had focused on either providing a high-level business-oriented view of processes or an executable view of business processes, they converged to providing both.

Initially, the Business Process Modeling Notation (BPMN) lacked a foundation for automating the orchestration and execution of services, as well as, a semantic foundation [17], but BPMN 2.0 has improved upon the situation. The latest standardization of the Business Process Modeling Notation (BPMN), BPMN 2.02, has seen a convergence of process modeling tools adopting this standard, including YAWL, jBPM, Camunda, Activiti, Bonita BPM, and Process Maker, see [25] for a more complete list and comparison.

BPMN 2.0 has three types of diagrams: business process diagram, conversation diagram, and choreography diagram [1]. The main diagram for process design is the business process diagram consisting of 4 types of elements [1,47]:

1. A Flow Object represents a vertex and may be an activity, event, or gateway.
2. A Connecting Object represents an edge connecting vertices.
3. A Partition is a collection of process elements where they gather in pools and move through swimlanes.
4. Artifacts include the data objects and data stores.

3.2   The Time Element in BPMN

Time is an important element in business process modeling [9]. There can be temporal constraints and dependencies as well as estimates for how long steps and whole processes will take. BPMN allows time to be given as properties or temporal constraints. For example, the completion of an activity may have a duration constraint. Timer events may be used to trigger actions or to take corrective measures.

Research efforts have expanded the use of time in processes. Time-BPMN [16] supports temporal constraints and dependencies between process activities, while [27] adds specification with mappings to Timed-Automata and [19] uses Timed-Petri-Nets. These allow for formal verification and model checking [9].

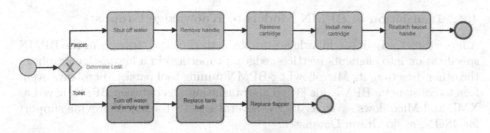

Fig. 1. Business process diagram for fixing two types of leaks.

3.3 Process Mining

Process mining can be used for process improvement. Data is mined from various sources including execution logs and user access logs to perform analysis on the business process. The analysis may involve predicting the next activity or the time it will take to complete the activity. Recently, deep learning techniques have been applied to the problem of predictive process mining [42].

4 Use of Knowledge Graphs in Process Modeling

The use of Knowledge Graphs in Process Modeling can be at several levels. For example, the use of Knowledge Graphs with business processes is argued in [10], which uses RDF for process model data sources. One may also provide semantic annotations to link elements in a process model (e.g., in BPMN) to a knowledge graph. Further, tools can be used/developed for translating from a BPMN representation (e.g., serialized in XML or JSON) to (or from) a Knowledge Graph. Finally, enhancements to Knowledge Graphs may allow organizations to fully store their business processes as part of their EKG.

4.1 Annotation of BPMN Models Using Knowledge Graphs

Much as WSDL-S [4] and SAWSDL were designed for adding semantic annotations to Web service descriptions/definitions and their compositions, BPMN specifications can be annotated by linking to concepts in Enterprise Knowledge Graphs.

Microflows [31] uses semantic annotation of micro-services via JSON-LD to provide an agile means for creating light-weight, dynamic business processes. It maps activities/micro-services to vertices in a graph storable in a graph database. Edges represent the flow between activities/micro-services. Microflows [31] uses the B2J tool to extract information from BPMN 2.0 files.

In [37], the functional and non-functional features of micro-services are described in knowledge graphs accessible as SPARQL endpoints.

4.2   Translation of BPMN Models to Knowledge Graphs

A more direct way to use knowledge graphs is to translate/transform the BPMN specification into elements (vertices, edges, properties) in a knowledge graph. In the other direction, its MicroflowLog-BPMN mining tool parses Microflows event logs to construct a BPMN file [31]. The translation was between BPMN saved as XML and Microflows saved as JSON. Several BPMN tools now provide support for JSON, as do Graph Databases.

The intersection of knowledge representation and business process modeling is addressed in [39]. A converter is developed to translate XML serializations of BPMN process models into knowledge graphs in the form Neo4j Labeled Property Graphs (LPGs). As a graph database, Neo4j aligns more closely with the graphical nature of BPMN as opposed to the hierarchical nature of XML. The Cypher query language also allows for more convenient search and navigation through process models. In [39], Fig. 1 shows a BPMN process, and Fig. 2 shows its translation drawn as a graph by Neo4j (see the Case Study later in this paper for analogous diagrams). A similar tool called BPMN2KG is presented in [6]. In this case, the Knowledge Graph is of the RDF/SPARQL variety instead of LPG/Cypher (note, Neosemantics links LPG with RDF). As multiple design languages/notations are used in software engineering including UML, SysML, and BPMN, [23] discuss how ontologies can serve as a common formalism.

Depending on their needs, an organization may choose to represent their process models as part of their Enterprise Knowledge Graph (see the Case Study later in this paper).

5   Application of Machine Learning

Over the last couple of decades, algorithms have been developed to help design and improve business processes [2]. Recent research has applied machine learning to these tasks. The fact that a business process can be represented as a graph, has allowed extensive research on knowledge graphs to be applied to process modeling and mining as highlighted below.

5.1   Subgraph Pattern Matching

Finding suitable subprocesses can be helpful in the design or improvement of business process models. Traditional algorithms for finding matching subgraphs in a large labeled graph include subgraph isomorphism, graph homomorphism, and various forms of graph simulation. Recently, machine learning techniques have been applied to further speed up graph pattern matching (both subgraph isomorphism and graph homomorphism are NP-Hard).

Reusability of process models or parts of process models can aid in the design of processes and help designers follow established best practices. In [34], BPMN models are treated as directed attributed graphs to which sub-graph isomorphism is applied to find reusable subprocesses. Using structural constraints such as Single-Entry, Single Exit (SESE) for regions of the process graph, implies the algorithm will run faster.

Although progress has been made in developing algorithms with improved average case performance, recent research has utilized machine learning to find approximate solutions more quickly. As subgraph isomorphism is also Approx-Hard, this is also very challenging. In [13], Graph Neural Networks are used to find matches two orders of magnitude more quickly than exact matching techniques. The matches found (although not exact) are substantially more accurate than other approximation (technically heuristic) techniques.

5.2 Knowledge Graph Completion

Building or composing business processes is a complex task. This can involve making an abstract process and finding activities or service invocations that can be used for a step in the abstract process. There has been substantial work on this, including service discovery for composition, service matching algorithms, and recommender systems. A related problem is to expand an existing (partially designed) business process by finding an activity to expand it. A new take is to use knowledge graph completion for recommending activities [35].

5.3 Knowledge Graph Embedding

One way to use a knowledge graph with machine learning is to represent the vertices as vectors in d-dimensional space. Each vertex $v \in V$ has an associated vector $\mathbf{v} \in \mathbb{R}^d$. These vectors may be placed randomly in space, but are interactively repositioned so that, for example, a relation/predicate p between two vertices (u, v), is mimicked in the vector space by having a vector for the relation $\mathbf{p}$ translate vector $\mathbf{u}$ to vector $\mathbf{v}$, i.e., $\mathbf{u} + \mathbf{p} = \mathbf{v}$.

The training via a loss function based on the norm of the difference $\|\mathbf{u}+\mathbf{p}-\mathbf{v}\|$ can be used to capture the structure of the graph in the vector space. This is called Translation Embedding or TransE [7,28,43] After training, the existence of a new triple (u, p, v) may be predicted when $\mathbf{u} + \mathbf{p} \approx \mathbf{v}$. In addition, the representations (vectors) can be fed into a machine-learning model, in order to improve that model's predictions.

For process modeling, temporal knowledge graph embedding may be more suitable. Embedding takes place on the quads (s, p, o, t) and can address several queries that can be used to fill in missing information, such as $(?, p, o, t)$ or $(s, p, ?, t)$ for missing entities, $(s, ?, o, t)$ for unknown relations/predicates, and $(s, p, o, ?)$ for unknown timestamps [8]. This can be particularly relevant to processes, for example, predicting the behavior of partially completed processes [21] or predicting how the process may evolve. Better tools, merged steps, increased automation, etc. may all be part of process improvement. Several enhancements to TransE are proposed in [21] to provide better embeddings of temporal knowledge graphs to be used for predicting process behavior.

A new direction for this research is to make timestamp predictions for future times (forecasting) or unseen past timestamps (imputation or backcasting). Various techniques have been used to capture the dynamics of entities in the temporal knowledge graph [8].

5.4 Graph Neural Networks

While Graph Embedding captures the structure and information content of Knowledge Graphs for use in machine learning models, Graph Neural Networks allow modeling to be performed directly on the knowledge graph, or a graph derived from, for example, the main enterprise knowledge graph.

A Graph Neural Network (GNN) works by updating the state of each vertex (neuron) based on its current value and an aggregation of values from it neighbors. Its flexible connection structure or topology is more similar to brain connections than other types of neural networks.

In [42], a comparison of multiple deep learning models used for process mining is conducted. A process is mined from the event logs by building a Directly-Follows Graph. From this an adjacency matrix A is constructed, normalized using the out-degree matrix D, multiplied by the feature matrix X as well as a trainable weight/parameter matrix W. In particular, they compared variants of Graph Convolution Networks (GCNs) with Convolution Neural Networks (CNNs), Long Short-Term Memory models (LSTMs), Generative Adversarial Nets (GANs), and Fully-Connected Neural Networks (FcNNs). Although GCN performed well for some of their experiments, overall results did not show a clear winner, suggesting that further research is needed.

An Encoder-Decoder Graph Neural Network is developed in [12] from a temporal knowledge graph and shown to produce good results for link prediction. Neighborhoods take into consideration the temporal dimension and thus affect the results of aggregation.

In [32], the authors address the problem of whether machine learning and in particular GNNs can be used to assist process model designers using existing process models to learn process model patterns. Time prediction or forecasting in temporal knowledge graphs is very challenging. The quads in a temporal knowledge graph may be thought of as discrete events and ordered by time (like a time series). Unlike a Poisson Process where the timings of events are independent, a Hawkes Process allows an event to excite future events. The Graph Hawkes Neural Network (GHNN) [18] combines the neighborhood aggregation capabilities of GNNs with a Hawkes process for predicting future events. It can make time as well as link predictions. They show that for link prediction, GHNN performs better than T-TransE, TA-TransE, TA-Dimult, Know-Evolve, and RE-Net [18].

5.5 Predictive Process Monitoring

Predictive process monitoring makes forecasts of the future of a process that is currently executing, including the type and time of future events as well as outcomes of the process. ProcK [20] feeds process event logs into deep learning architectures in the form of Graph Neural Networks and Sequential Models. The event logs are complemented by a knowledge graph that includes information about process inputs or business/transactional knowledge. Due to the large size of the event logs, ProcK does not model everything as events/quads as in temporal knowledge graphs, rather it maintains this complementary information.

6   Case Studies

The first case study illustrates how a process model can be created from multiple sources and tied into an Enterprise Knowledge Graph, while the second one (in the appendix) highlights how analytics can be applied to a process model.

6.1   Do It Yourself Projects

Do It Yourself (DIY) projects can be supported by maintaining process models and supporting information. When they are maintained in Temporal Knowledge Graphs they may be linked to Enterprise Knowledge Graphs.

DIY projects can be supported by Web Service Processes or Apps, that can customize the help provided to the customer. It can recommend tools and products needed for the project, taking into account the users' preferences. The core of the project can be modeled as a process and event logs may be maintained on the customer's progress. Although the basic process can be presented to the customer ahead of time in the form of instructions, YouTube videos, or process diagrams, process mining, and monitoring can provide further assistance, in the form of suggesting the next activity in case the process has multiple branches, predicting how long this next step will take (with customized timing for the current customer) and even troubleshooting when something unexpected happens.

Generally speaking, DIY project information consists of both structured and unstructured text segments, documents, videos, etc. describing the steps involved. To make a knowledge graph from such inputs, the following steps can be followed:

Re-use or modify an existing ontology that fits with the domain: schema.org has a collection of standard ontologies. For example, the "HowTo" schema that comes under "CreativeWork" should be a good fit as an ontology of a process for DIY projects. Many processes need a set of tools/products and those can be described with the "product" schema and linked with "HowTo" via the property named "material". The ontology may need to be adjusted to completely align with the domain. There exists software like Protégé [29] for tailoring ontology. In Fig. 2, the blue and purple nodes represent steps and they can be linked with "HowTo" schema via the "steps" property. Similarly "faucet", "tank ball" can be linked with the "product" ontology.

Perform named entity recognition on the dataset: Key entities are the distinct processes, individual steps of the process, tools needed in each step, etc. If

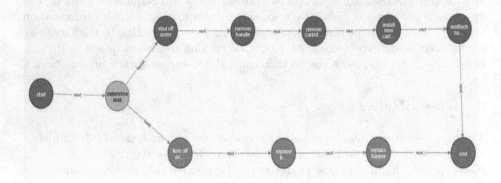

Fig. 2. Process model for fixing two types of leaks (Color figure online)

there exists a product catalog then standard text-matching algorithms like Aho-Corasick [3] can be leveraged to extract them. Nevertheless, extracting named entities from plain text can be challenging and the extractor has to acknowledge the context while processing texts to resolve ambiguity. A conditional random field model can be trained to extract the entities [15,45]. A rule-based classifier might also be effective if the text can be largely covered by a set of semantic and syntactic-lexical patterns [36]. Transformer-based approaches can also be effective to recognize entities [40].

Find relationship between the extracted entities: Several relationships between the entities are important to have a functioning and useful knowledge graph in this case study. For example, the order/topology of the steps, the association of tools/products with individual steps, etc. The order of the steps can be indicated in the knowledge graph with "followed by" or "next" relationship as shown in Fig. 2. Linking tools/products with each step should be trivial if the entities are correctly recognized. Graph embedding based knowledge graph completion techniques, such as TransE [7], TransH [44], TransR [22], ComplEx [38], etc., can be applied to extract learnable relationships between recognized entities. The Poincaré embedding can be more effective in this case for embedding given that it embeds the hierarchical structure of the nodes representing the ontology as well [46].

Make a natural language processor to convert user-provided queries to structured query (e.g., SPARQL): Such adapters make the knowledge graph user friendly and accessible. Dezhao et al. [36] converted natural language quries to First Order Logic (FOL). The logic is then parsed through a parse tree and an in-order traversal is performed to generate the structured query.

Appendix: COVID-19 as a Disease Process

A process model may be created for the COVID-19 disease as follows starting with a graph that represents the main states and state transitions.

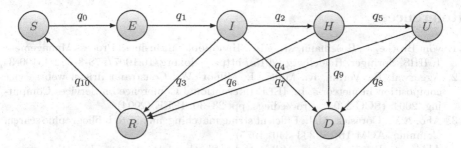

Fig. 3. State transition diagram for a SEIHURD model

The states are Susceptible (S), Exposed (E), Infected (I), Hospitalized (H), Intensive Care Unit (U), Recovered (R), and Died (D). From patient data timestamps may be attached to each state. From these, durations may be attached to edges, e.g., positive test $\implies$ infected, and after say 6 d the patient is hospitalized, after 4 d, the patient is placed in the unit, etc. Similar time annotations may be used for aggregated data (at national and state levels) such as that provided by the Centers for Disease Control and Prevention (CDC), Johns Hopkins University (JHU), or Our World in Data (OWID).

Analytics may be performed by maintaining population counts for each of the vertices and transition rates (alternatively expected transition times) between vertices/states. A variety of modeling techniques may be applied, including Continuous-Time Markov Chains, Compartmental models (a system of ordinary differential equations), Vector Auto-Regressive (VAR) models, Staged Seasonal, Auto-Regressive, Integrated, Moving Average, Exogenous (SARIMAX) models, and several types of Deep Learning models.

A type of deep learning model that is showing potential for capturing much of the dynamics of the disease process is Graph Neural Network (GNN) model. A GNN can be built from Multivariate Time-Series (MTS) where each of the $n = 7$ variables forms a column in matrix Y. Given that these variables (and others) for COVID-19 have been recorded daily since January 2020, there are now about $m = 1000$ rows of data, so $Y \in \mathbb{R}^{m \times n}$. Each element in matrix Y, y_{tj} where t is time/day and j designates which variable, e.g., $j = 2 \implies$ I, forms a vertex in the GNN. Contemporaneous (at the same time) edges may be added based on the state-transition graph, they should be labeled as contemporaneous as these data/counts may not be available for forecasting. Structural learning should be performed to determine adjacency. Edges in the GNN can be added and removed by learning from data, for example, by associative or causal analysis between vertices using cross-correlation, Granger causality, or cross-mutual information. The most correlated or causal edges should be added (e.g., H $\rightarrow$ D preliminary analysis shows strong lagged effects at 8 and 14 d). A generic GNN for MTS forecasting is given in [11]; see Fig. 1 for a depiction of what such a GNN would look like. Research into the modeling and analysis of such processes can cross fertilize research into business processes.

References

1. vom Brocke, J., Rosemann, M. (eds.): Handbook on Business Process Management 1. IHIS, Springer, Heidelberg (2015). https://doi.org/10.1007/978-3-642-45100-3
2. Aggarwal, R., Verma, K., Miller, J., Milnor, W.: Constraint driven web service composition in meteor-s. In: IEEE International Conference on Services Computing, 2004. (SCC 2004), Proceedings, pp. 23–30. IEEE (2004)
3. Aho, A.V., Corasick, M.J.: Efficient string matching: an aid to bibliographic search. Commun. ACM **18**(6), 333–340 (1975)
4. Akkiraju, R., Farrell, J., Miller, J.A., Sheth, A.P., Verma, K.: Web service semantics-wsdl-s, Meenakshi Nagarajan (2005)
5. Andrews, T., et al.: Business process execution language for web services, Doug Smith (2003)
6. Bachhofner, S., Kiesling, E., Revoredo, K., Waibel, P., Polleres, A.: Automated process knowledge graph construction from BPMN models. In: Strauss, C., Cuzzocrea, A., Kotsis, G., Tjoa, A.M., Khalil, I. (eds) Database and Expert Systems Applications. DEXA 2022. LNCS, vol. 13426. Springer, Cham (2022). https://doi.org/10.1007/978-3-031-12423-5_3
7. Bordes, A., Usunier, N., Garcia-Duran, A., Weston, J., Yakhnenko, O.: Translating embeddings for modeling multi-relational data. In: Advances in Neural Information Processing Systems 26 (2013)
8. Cai, B., Xiang, Y., Gao, L., Zhang, H., Li, Y., Li, J.: Temporal knowledge graph completion: a survey. arXiv preprint arXiv:2201.08236 (2022)
9. Cheikhrouhou, S., Kallel, S., Guermouche, N., Jmaiel, M.: The temporal perspective in business process modeling: a survey and research challenges. SOCA **9**(1), 75–85 (2015)
10. Cinpoeru, M., Ghiran, A.-M., Harkai, A., Buchmann, R.A., Karagiannis, D.: Model-driven context configuration in business process management systems: an approach based on knowledge graphs. In: Pańkowska, M., Sandkuhl, K. (eds.) BIR 2019. LNBIP, vol. 365, pp. 189–203. Springer, Cham (2019). https://doi.org/10.1007/978-3-030-31143-8_14
11. Cui, Y., et al.: METRO: a generic graph neural network framework for multivariate time series forecasting. Proc. VLDB Endowment **15**(2), 224–236 (2021)
12. Ding, Z., Ma, Y., He, B., Tresp, V.: A simple but powerful graph encoder for temporal knowledge graph completion. arXiv:2112.07791 (2021)
13. Duong, C.T., Hoang, T.D., Yin, H., Weidlich, M., Nguyen, Q.V.H., Aberer, K: Efficient streaming subgraph isomorphism with graph neural networks. Proc. VLDB Endowment **14**(5), 730–742 (2021)
14. Fensel, D., et al.: Introduction: what is a knowledge graph? In: Knowledge Graphs, pp. 1–10. Springer, Cham (2020). https://doi.org/10.1007/978-3-030-37439-6_1
15. Finkel, J.R., Grenager, T., Manning, C.D: Incorporating non-local information into information extraction systems by gibbs sampling. In Proceedings of the 43rd Annual Meeting of the Association for Computational Linguistics (ACL2005), pp. 363–370 (2005)
16. Gagne, D., Trudel, A.: Time-BPMN. In: 2009 IEEE conference on commerce and enterprise computing, pp. 361–367. IEEE (2009)
17. Grolinger, K., Capretz, M.A.M., Cunha, A., Tazi, S.: Integration of business process modeling and web services: a survey. SOCA. **8**(2), 105–128 (2014)
18. Han, Z., Wang, Y., Ma, Y., Günnemann, S., Tresp, V.: Graph Hawkes network for reasoning on temporal knowledge graphs. arXiv:2003.13432 (2020)

19. Huai, W., Liu, X., Sun, X.: Towards trustworthy composite service through business process model verification. In: 2010 7th International Conference on Ubiquitous Intelligence Computing and 7th International Conference on Autonomic Trusted Computing, pp. 422–427. IEEE (2010)

20. Jacobs, T., Yu, J., Gastinger, J., Sztyler, T.: Prock: machine learning for knowledge-intensive processes. arXiv:2109.04881 (2021)

21. Karetnikov, A., Ehrlinger, L., Geist, V.: Enhancing transe to predict process behavior in temporal knowledge graphs. In: Database and Expert Systems Applications - DEXA 2022 Workshops. DEXA 2022. Communications in Computer and Information Science, vol. 1633. Springer, Cham (2022). https://doi.org/10.1007/978-3-031-14343-4_34

22. Lin, Y., Liu, Z., Sun, M., Liu, Y., Zhu, X.: Learning entity and relation embeddings for knowledge graph completion. In: Twenty-ninth AAAI Conference on Artificial Intelligence (2015)

23. Lu, J., Ma, J., Zheng, X., Wang, G., Li, H., Kiritsis, D.: Design ontology supporting model-based systems engineering formalisms. IEEE Syst. J. 1–12 (2021)

24. Lu, R., Sadiq, S.: A survey of comparative business process modeling approaches. In: Abramowicz, W. (ed.) BIS 2007. LNCS, vol. 4439, pp. 82–94. Springer, Heidelberg (2007). https://doi.org/10.1007/978-3-540-72035-5_7

25. Meidan, A., García-García, J.A., Escalona, M.J., Ramos, I.: A survey on business processes management suites. Comput. Stan. Interfaces 51, 71–86 (2017)

26. Mendling, J., Nüttgens, M.: EPC markup language (EPML): an xml-based interchange format for event-driven process chains (EPC). ISEB 4(3), 245–263 (2006)

27. Morales, L.E.M.: Business process verification: the application of model checking and timed automata. CLEI Electron. J. 17(2), 3–3 (2014)

28. Minervini, P., d'Amato, C., Fanizzi, N., Esposito, F.: Efficient learning of entity and predicate embeddings for link prediction in knowledge graphs. URSW@ ISWC, 1479, 26–37 (2015)

29. Musen, M.A.: The protégé project: a look back and a look forward. AI Matters 1(4), 4–12 (2015)

30. Noy, N., Gao, Y., Jain, A., Narayanan, A., Patterson, A., Taylor, J.: Industry-scale knowledge graphs: lessons and challenges: five diverse technology companies show how it's done. Queue 17(2), 48–75 (2019)

31. Oberhauser, R., Stigler, S.: Microflows: enabling agile business process modeling to orchestrate semantically-annotated microservices. In: Seventh International Symposium on Business Modeling and Software Design (BMSD 2017), vol. 1, pp. 19–28 (2017)

32. Serral, E., Stirna, J., Ralyté, J., Grabis, J. (eds.): PoEM 2021. LNBIP, vol. 432. Springer, Cham (2021). https://doi.org/10.1007/978-3-030-91279-6

33. Simsek, U., Angele, K., Kärle, E., Opdenplatz, J., Sommer, D., Umbrich, J., Fensel, D.: Building and maintaining knowledge graphs, Knowledge graph lifecycle (2021)

34. Skouradaki, M., Göerlach, K., Hahn, M., Leymann, F.: Application of sub-graph isomorphism to extract reoccurring structures from BPMN 2.0 process models. In: 2015 IEEE Symposium on Service-Oriented System Engineering, pp. 11–20. IEEE (2015)

35. Sola, D., Meilicke, C., van der Aa, H., Stuckenschmidt, H.: On the use of knowledge graph completion methods for activity recommendation in business process modeling. In: Marrella, A., Weber, B. (eds.) BPM 2021. LNBIP, vol. 436, pp. 5–17. Springer, Cham (2022). https://doi.org/10.1007/978-3-030-94343-1_1

36. Song, D., et al.: Building and querying an enterprise knowledge graph. IEEE Trans. Serv. Comput. 12(3), 356–369 (2017)

37. Steindl, G., Kastner, W.: Semantic microservice framework for digital twins. Appl. Sci. **11**(12), 5633 (2021)
38. Trouillon, T., Welbl, J., Riedel, S., Gaussier, É., Bouchard, G.: Complex embeddings for simple link prediction. In: International Conference on Machine Learning, pp. 2071–2080. PMLR (2016)
39. Uifălean, S., Ghiran, A.-M., Buchmann, R.A.: From BPMN models to labelled property graphs. in information systems development: artificial intelligence for information systems development and operations (ISD2022) (2022)
40. Ushio, A., Camacho-Collados, J.: T-NER: an all-round python library for transformer-based named entity recognition. arXiv preprint arXiv:2209.12616 (2022)
41. van der Aalst, W.M.P., Ter Hofstede, A.H.M.: Yawl: yet another workflow language. Inf. syst. **30**(4), 245–275 (2005)
42. Venugopal, I., Töllich, J., Fairbank, M., Scherp, A.: A comparison of deep-learning methods for analysing and predicting business processes. In: 2021 International Joint Conference on Neural Networks (IJCNN), pp. 1–8. IEEE (2021)
43. Wang, Q., Mao, Z., Wang, B., Guo, L.: Knowledge graph embedding: a survey of approaches and applications. IEEE Trans. Knowl. Data Eng. **29**(12), 2724–2743 (2017)
44. Wang, Z., Zhang, J., Feng, J., Chen, Z.: Knowledge graph embedding by translating on hyperplanes. In: Proceedings of the AAAI Conference on Artificial Intelligence, vol. 28 (2014)
45. Wu, S., Fang, Z., Tang, J.: Accurate product name recognition from user generated content. In: 2012 IEEE 12th International Conference on Data Mining Workshops, pp. 874–877. IEEE (2012)
46. Xu, D., Ruan, C., Korpeoglu, E., Kumar, S., Achan, K.: Product knowledge graph embedding for e-commerce. In: Proceedings of the 13th International Conference on Web Search and Data Mining, pp. 672–680 (2020)
47. Zarour, K., Benmerzoug, D., Guermouche, N., Drira, K.: A systematic literature review on BPMN extensions. Bus. Process Manage. J. **26**(6), 1473–1503 (2019)

Boosting Item Coverage in Session-Based Recommendation

Richard Anarfi[1], Amartya Sen[2], and Kenneth K. Fletcher[1]([✉])

[1] University of Massachusetts Boston, Boston, MA 02125, USA
{richard.anarfi001,kenneth.fletcher}@umb.edu
[2] Oakland University, Rochester, MI 48309, USA
sen@oakland.edu

Abstract. Traditional recommender systems that rely heavily on user profiles or historical consumption of users are more susceptible to the cold start and model drift limitations due to dynamic user preferences. Recent advances in recommendations have seen a shift towards session-based recommender systems, which provide recommendations solely based on a user's interactions in an ongoing session. As a result, the focus is placed on sequential learning, and existing algorithms are heavily impacted by accidental clicks, which ultimately limits an item's coverage. In this work, we propose a two-stage approach to boosting item's coverage in session-based recommendations. First, we train a skip-gram model with negative sampling to generate candidate items that co-occur with a given query set. We then apply weighting to mitigate the effects of accidental clicks during a session. Next, we use a multi-armed bandit approach to boost recommendation coverage by balancing the exploration-exploitation trade-off. Experiments with three real-world datasets show that our model's performance is comparable to existing state-of-the-art methods and outperforms them in recommendation coverage.

Keywords: Reinforcement learning · word2vec · Recommender systems · Language modeling · Deep learning

1 Introduction

Recommendation systems (RS) aim to improve user experience by aiding users sift through massive online platforms to discover new products and services [1]. This is done via information filtering, aiming at personalizing and improving user experience, typically through a learned user profile. Approaches to RS are usually categorized as content-based, collaborative filtering, or hybrid variants that combine aspects of the above two categories. The past few years have seen a shift towards session-based RS. These systems [25] make recommendations for a user solely based on their interactions in an ongoing session. Session-based RS provides several benefits including alleviating the cold start limitation [8] and capturing dynamic preferences [22,23], which can be masked by a dependency on historic sessions.

In light of these numerous recommendation system types available, an important research question is: *What is a good RS?* Several metrics [12] have been proposed to evaluate the performance of RS. Accuracy metrics like Mean Reciprocal Rank (MRR) and Hit Rate (HR) highly reward recommendation algorithms that focus on solely exploiting the learned user profile. Beyond these accuracy metrics, other quality metrics [20] like coverage, novelty, and diversity can be equally important depending on the domain.

Coverage is a fraction that represents the possible recommendations that an RS can generate. What makes it essential is that it gives an idea of how quickly a new item or an item with very few recorded interactions can show up in a recommendation list. In order to boost coverage, some works consider serendipity, also known as the element of surprise. Previous studies have shown that this approach usually comes with its trade-offs [9]. If the recommendations made through serendipity cause a bad user experience, the RS will lose its essence [32]. For this reason, in this work, we propose a method to boost coverage of items in a session-based RS.

1.1   Motivation

One of the main motivations of this work is to investigate the performance of existing session-based RS in light of item coverage and then explore how it relates to some other accuracy metrics. For this reason, we carried out a preliminary study to assess the item coverage of current state-of-the-art session-based RS. Our case study is from a comprehensive survey [24] of session-based RS. An excerpt from exploratory data analysis of the performance results is shown here in Fig. 1. The figure shows a plot of Mean Reciprocal Rank (MRR) and Coverage (COV) for a recommendation list length of 20 items on the RCS15 dataset. We observed that item co-occurrence played a key role since about 80% of the items that were not covered in the predictions had very few session

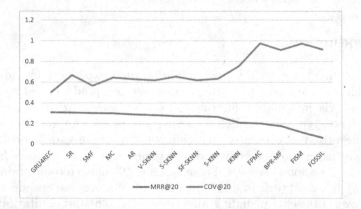

Fig. 1. A plot of Mean Reciprocal Rank (MRR) and Coverage (COV) for a recommendation list length of 20 items.

interactions. It appears that existing session-based RS sacrifice coverage in favor of recommendation accuracy.

1.2   Contributions

Our main contributions for this work is as follows:

- We pre-train a Bidirectional Encoder Representations from Transformers (BERT) language model with a focus on the next sentence prediction (NSP) task. We use this model to score dependencies across items consumed in a session. We refer to this model as the session ranker.
- We train a skip-gram word2vec model with negative sampling to capture the semantic relationship between items via item embedding. We make next item queries on a query set in a user session to mitigate the effect of an accidental click when using only the last item as the query item. We re-rank the candidate items using the session ranker.
- We carry out an epsilon-greedy multi-armed bandit approach to balance the exploitation-exploration trade-off. We boost item coverage by sampling from low frequency items in the environment. The reward signal for each action item is obtained from the session ranker.

2   Background

2.1   Word Embeddings

This section summarizes the work of Mikolov et al. [27] for learning distributed representations of words. For the CBOW architecture, the non-linear hidden layer is removed and the projection layer is shared for all words and not just the projection matrix. Instead of predicting the current word based on the context, the continuous skip-gram model tries to maximize the classification of a word based on another word in the same sentence. Each current word is used as an input to a log-linear classifier with a continuous projection layer and predicts words within a certain range before and after the current word.

2.2   BERT Language Model

Devlin et al. [5] introduced BERT, which stands for Bidirectional Encoder Representations from Transformers. It was designed to alleviate the unidirectional constraint of previous transformer architectures. The major portion of BERT is a very large multi-layer bidirectional Transformer encoder [36] which comprises of a 12-layer neural network that processes text. Figure 2 shows the BERT input representation.

Pre-training and fine-tuning are the two steps in the BERT framework. Pre-training consists of two unsupervised tasks known as Masked Language Modeling (MLM) and Next Sentence Prediction (NSP). In MLM, a percentage of the input tokens are masked at random and the goal is to predict these masked tokens. In

NSP, the relationship between two sentences is explored. When choosing the sentences for each pre-training example, actual sentences that follow are chosen 50% of the time and random sentences are chosen the remaining time. Fine-tuning allows for transfer learning to occur. The pre-trained model weights are used in modeling several downstream tasks. This is made possible by the self-attention mechanism in the transformer and also the flexibility in swapping out the appropriate inputs and outputs to tailor the model to the specific downstream task.

2.3   Exploration and Exploitation

One of the most important challenges in reinforcement learning (RL)-based recommendation [2,3] is the trade-off that the learning agent has to make between exploration and exploitation [34]. The agent has the fundamental choice of gathering more information through new actions in hopes of finding better ways to maximize expected rewards or stick with actions that are previously known good decisions.

A Multi-Armed Bandit problem [7] is a sequential decision problem where an algorithm continually chooses among a set of possible actions referred to as arms. Contextual bandit tasks [16] are intermediate between n-armed bandit problems and a full RL problem. It focuses on immediate rewards like n-armed bandit problems. It also follows an agent policy in a typical RL setup for selecting actions by using contextual information.

In order to obtain the maximum reward, the agent prefers to take an action that likely to return the optimal reward by determining the experiences from the past. However, by acting greedy at all time, the agent will not learn any new information. Correspondingly, to discover the optimal decision, the agent learns from trial-and-error. Thereby, the agent has to exploit to obtain the expected optimal reward, but it also has to explore new actions to learn which action return optimal reward in the future.

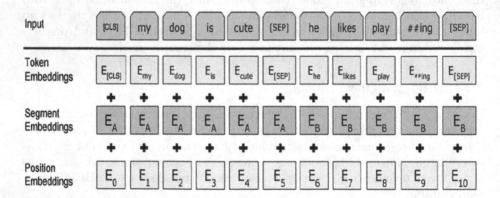

Fig. 2. BERT input representation. The input embeddings are the sum of the token embeddings, the segmentation embeddings and the position embeddings [5].

3   Related Works

This section discusses related works in recommendation systems with a focus on word2vec, multi-armed bandits, session-based recommendation and item coverage.

3.1   Word2vec for Recommendation

Esmeli et al. [6] integrated product similarities as a feature of classification models to improve prediction accuracy. They calculated product similarities using Word2Vec method, in which the session represents the sentence, and the product id represents the words in the sentence. They chose items in different positions in a session to find the best combination for the best purchase prediction accuracy. To make hyperparameter optimization applicable for large scale recommendation problems where the target dataset is too large to search over, Chamberlain et al. [4] investigate generalizing hyperparameters settings from samples. They show that applying constrained hyperparameter optimization using only a 10% sample of the data still yields a 91% average improvement in hit rate over the default parameters when applied to the full datasets used in their work.

3.2   Multi-armed Bandits for Recommendation

Zeng et al. [39] studied the time varying contextual multi-armed problem where the reward mapping function changes over time. They propose a dynamical context drift model based on particle learning. The drift on the reward mapping function is explicitly modeled as a set of random walk particles, where good fitted particles are selected to learn the mapping dynamically. Sanz-Cruzado et al. [31] developed a multi-armed neighbor-based bandit approach that achieves effective collaborative filtering when recommendation is understood to be an interactive process with a feedback loop. Their approach is sensitive to the uncertainty in the available observations of user-user preference similarity, modeling this uncertainty in a well-established stochastic scheme.

3.3   Session-Based Recommendation

Tan et al. [35] study recurrent neural network-based models for session-based recommendations. They propose the application of data augmentation, and a method to account for shifts in the input data distribution. They also empirically study the use of generalized distillation, and an alternative model that directly predicts item embeddings. Greenstein-Messica et al. [11] evaluated the effectiveness of using state of the art word embedding methods GloVe and Word2Vec for e-commerce. They claimed that using item embedding vectors, as a compressed meaningful input representation will be efficient for various recommender system applications. Wu et al. [37] presents an architecture for session-based recommendation that incorporates graph models into representing session sequences. Their method not only considers the complex structure and transitions between items of session sequences, but also develops a strategy to combine long-term preferences and current interests of sessions to better predict users' next actions.

3.4   Coverage in Recommendation

Ge et al. [9] discuss both measurement methods as well as the trade-off between good coverage and serendipity. They then analyze the role of coverage and serendipity as indicators of recommendation quality, present ways of how they can be measured and discuss how to interpret the obtained measurements. Collaborative Filtering with Clustering ReRanking Technique was proposed by Zuva et al. [40]. Their method aims to improve the recommendation quality by re-ranking the recommended list in such that long-tail items are represented. Maccatrozzo et al. [26] presented a model for serendipity in content-based recommender system inspired by curiosity theories. They show that novelty check and coping potential check are essential aspects of the serendipitous assessment. Neural Serendipity Recommendation method was proposed by Xu et al. [38]. They combined Muti-Layer Percetron and Matrix Factorization for serendipity prediction and used a weighted candidate filtering method for personalized recommendation. Kawamae et al. [21] show the impact of trends on the transition probability of items, and that the estimated time offset to purchase in the absence of recommendations is a useful metric of serendipitousness. They offer improvements on the user-item coverage, the Gini coefficient, the elapsed time, the difference in estimated time, and the predictive performance.

4   Proposed Model

In this section we give a detailed walk through of our proposed model which we refer to as Coverage Bandit (COV-BDT). We start by outlining the problem definition and build up to our model architecture. We then discuss the elements of our modular model which consists of a session ranker, a skip-gram with negative sampling (SGNS) model and an epsilon-greedy model.

Let $U = \{u_1, u_2, ..., u_n\}$ be a set of n users and $I = \{I_1, I_2, ..., I_{|I|}\}$ be a set of items. For a given user u_i, where $1 \leq i \leq n$, we denote the ongoing user session as $S^{u_i} = \{I_1^{u_i}, ..., I_t^{u_i}\}$. $I_t^{u_i}$ refers to user u_i consuming item I_t at interaction timestep t. Given the interaction history S^{u_i}, in an ongoing session predict the item that user u_i will interact with at interaction time step $t + 1$.

We first describe the architecture of our model as shown in Fig. 3 which we will refer to as the COV-Greedy model. Then we will highlight on the key elements of our model which consists of a trained skip-gram model, an ϵ-greedy bandit and a session ranker. To boost coverage, we also build a coverage map with existing session information. This consists of a dictionary with items as keys and their frequency of occurrence across sessions as values.

Algorithm 1 shows the sequence of steps we take to carry out the next item recommendation task for an ongoing session. To measure coherence across continuing session fragments we pre-train a BERT language model and carry out

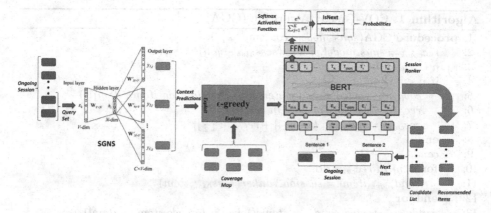

Fig. 3. Overview of the proposed model for session-based recommendation

inference on the Next Sentence Prediction task with ordered session fragments. The embedding of each candidate item is used as the last word piece with which a probability score is extracted for comparison with other candidates. We refer to this model as the *session ranker*.

For a query set from an ongoing session, we generate context predictions for each target item in the query set. These context predictions are observed by an ϵ-greedy bandit which decides to exploit the predictions with a probability of $1 - \epsilon$ or carry out exploration with a probability of ϵ by invoking the coverage map. If the bandit decides to carry out exploitation, the context predictions are chosen one after the other and are re-ranked according to their probability of continuing the session in a next sentence prediction task. On the other hand, if the bandit decides to explore, then we reduce the query set elements by one and fetch candidates to augment the context predictions from the coverage map. In a similar fashion to the exploitation case, these are also re-ranked according to their probability of continuing the session in a next sentence prediction task.

4.1   Session Ranker

The session ranker is essentially a pre-trained BERT model that does inference with the NSP task it has been trained on. As described by Sun et al. [33] we also adopt the multi-head self attention instead of performing a single attention function in our transformer layers.

Given an input session of length t, by applying the transformer layer [36], we compute hidden representations h_i^l to form a matrix H^l. For the first sub-layer, linear projections are made into h subspaces and the output representations are as shown below:

$$MH(H^l) = [head_1; head_2; ...; head_h]W^O \tag{1}$$

where $head_i = Attention(H^l W_i^Q, H^l W_i^K, H^l W_i^V)$. The projection matrices from each head are learnable parameters.

Algorithm 1. COV-Greedy Algorithm (CGA)

```
1: procedure CGA(sgns_model, cov_map, k, ε):
2:      rec_cand = sgns_model.predict(sess_hist[−q_l :])
3:      n ← rand(0, 1)
4:      if n < ε then:
5:          cov_list ← sorted(cov_map.items(), key = lambda item : item[1])
6:          rec_cov = [pair[0] for pair in cov_list]
7:          rec_cand = rec_cand[: k − ⌊k/2⌋] + rec_cov[: ⌊k/2⌋]
8:      end if
9:      cand_score ← {}
10:     for item in rec_cand do:
11:         cand_score[item] = session_ranker(sess_hist, item)
12:     end for
13:     cand_list ← sorted(cand_score.items(), key = lambda item : −item[1])
14:     rec_list = [pair[0] for pair in cand_list]
15:     for item in rec_list do:
16:         cov_map[item] += 1
17:     end for
18:     return rec_list
19: end procedure
```

The next sub-layer consists of a position-wise feed-forward network. This is applied separately and identically to each position with a RELU function in between two linear transformations.

$$FFN(x) = max(0, xW1 + b1)W2 + b2 \qquad (2)$$

4.2 Skip-Gram Model

The training objective of the Skip-gram model is to find word representations that are useful for predicting the surrounding words in a sentence or a document [27]. Given a predicted word vector $\hat{r}$ and a target word vector w_t. The probability of the target word conditional on the predicted word is calculated by a softmax function:

$$P(w_t|\hat{r}) = \frac{exp(w_t^T \hat{r})}{\sum_{w \in W} exp(w^T \hat{r})}$$

where W is the set of all target word vectors.

In training, word2vec models' cost functions aim to minimize the negative log-likelihood of the target word vector given its corresponding predicted word:

$$\mathcal{L}(w_t, \hat{r}) = -\log P(w_t|\hat{r}) = \log \left(\sum_{w \in W} exp(w^T \hat{r}) \right) - w_i^T \hat{r}$$

The gradient with respect to w of $\mathcal{L}(w_t, \hat{r})$ is:

$$g_1(w, w_t, W, \hat{r}) = \frac{\partial}{\partial w} \mathcal{L}(w_t, \hat{r}) = \hat{r}(P(w|\hat{r}) - I\{w = w_t\}) \qquad (3)$$

where I is the indicator function.

The gradient with respect to $\hat{r}$ is:

$$g_2(w_t, W, \hat{r}) = \frac{\partial}{\partial \hat{r}} \mathcal{L}(w_t, \hat{r}) = \sum_{w \in W} [P(w|\hat{r})w] - w_t \qquad (4)$$

For an index i and a window size c, skip-gram predicts the context words $\{w_j\}$, $(i - c \leq j \leq i + c, j \neq i)$ given the centered word r_i. Hence, in the general model, $w_t = w_j$ and $\hat{r} = r_i$.

Accordingly, the cost function is derived as follows:

$$\mathcal{L}_{skipgram}(c, i) = \sum_{i-c \leq j \leq i+c, i \neq j} - \log P(w_j|r_i)$$

The gradients of this function are:

$$\frac{\partial}{\partial w} \mathcal{L}_{skipgram}(c, i) = r_i \sum_{i-c \leq j \leq i+c, i \neq j} g_1(w, w_j, W, r_i) \qquad (5)$$

$$\frac{\partial}{\partial r_i} \mathcal{L}_{skipgram}(c, i) = \sum_{i-c \leq j \leq i+c, i \neq j} g_2(w_j, W, r_i) \qquad (6)$$

4.3 Epsilon-Greedy Model

We balance exploration and exploitation using ϵ-greedy policies. In relation to the quality of an action (a), suppose you form action value estimates such that at time-step t, $Q_t(a) \approx Q^*(a)$. The greedy action at t is given by:

$$a_t^* = \underset{a}{argmax} \, Q_t(a) \qquad (7)$$

During exploitation, the selected action:

$$a_t = a_t^* \qquad (8)$$

On the other hand, during exploration, the selected action:

$$a_t \neq a_t^* \qquad (9)$$

The optimal value of the parameter ϵ is typically problem-dependent, and found through experimentation. It is usually annealed over time in order to favor exploration at the beginning, and exploitation closer to convergence [10]. In our approach, we tune this parameter to suit the expected coverage. We make the effects of the bandit adaptive by updating the coverage map after each recommendation for a session.

5   Experiments

In this section, we perform experiments to evaluate our proposed method against state-of-the-art session-based recommendation systems.

Table 1. Statistical information of e-commerce datasets.

Dataset	RCS15	TMALL	RETAILR
Actions	5.43M	13.42M	212,182
Sessions	1.38M	1.77M	59,962
Items	28,582	425,348	31,968
Timespan in days	31	91	27
Actions per session	3.95	7.56	3.54
Unique items per session	3.17	5.56	2.56
Actions per day	175,063	149,096	7858
Sessions per day	44,358	19,719	2220

5.1 Datasets and Experimental Setup

The experiments were performed on three real world e-commerce datasets. RSC15 dataset was published in the context of the ACM RecSys 2015 Challenge and contains recorded click sequences for a period of six months. For RSC15, each split consists of 30 days of training and 1 day of test data. The TMALL dataset was published in the context of the TMall competition and contains interaction logs of the tmall.com website for one year. Each split consists of 90 days of training and 1 day of test data. The e-commerce personalization company retailrocket published the RETAILR dataset which covers six months of user browsing activities, also in the context of a competition. Each split consists of 25 days of training and 2 days of test data. Table 1 shows the statistical information of the above e-commerce datasets.

In pre-training the session ranker we set the maximum position embeddings parameter to 514, we use the default 12 attention heads from the original BERT training parameters, and choose 6 hidden layers. For the skip-gram model with negative sampling (SGNS), we set our embedding vector dimension to 100, the sliding window maximum length to 10, a 0.75 negative sampling exponent, 10 negative samples and 0.05 initial learning rate. For our experiments, we obtained the best results from our model by setting ϵ to 0.25.

5.2 Performance Evaluation

In this section, we highlight the state-of-the-art baselines we compared our model to and the metrics used for evaluation.

Baselines. The following baselines from Ludwig and Jannach [24] were used:

- **Simple Association Rules (AR)** [24]: This method captures the frequency of two co-occurring events. The rules and their corresponding importance are learned by finding the frequency with which two items occurred together in a session of any user.

- **Markov Chains (MC)** [28]: Here, the association rules are extracted from a first-order Markov Chain, which describes the transition probability between two subsequent events in a session. The frequency with which users viewed a specific item immediately after another is considered.
- **Sequential Rules (SR)** [19]: In contrast with the previous methods, a rule is created when an item appeared after another in a session even when other events happened between them.
- **Bayesian Personalized Ranking (BPR-MF)** [29]: Each session corresponds to a user in the user-item interaction matrix. The average of the latent item vectors of the current session so far as the user vector is used during prediction.
- **Item-based kNN (IKNN)** [15]: This method considers the last element in a given session and then returns those items as recommendations that are most similar by cosine similarity to it in terms of their co-occurrence in other sessions.
- **Session-based kNN (S-KNN)** [17]: This method compares the entire current session with the past sessions in the training data to determine the items to be recommended. Given a session, the most similar past sessions are determined by applying a session cosine similarity on binary vectors over the item space.
- **Vector Multiplication Session-Based kNN (V-SKNN)** [17]: This method uses real-valued vectors to encode the current session. The last element of the session obtains a value of 1 and the weights of the other elements are determined using a linear decay function that depends on the position of the element within the session.
- **Sequential Session-based kNN (S-SKNN)** [17]: This variant also puts more weight on elements that appear later in the session. Here, an indicator function is complemented with a weighting function, which takes the order of the events in the current session s into account. The weight increases when the more recent items of the current session also appears in a neighboring session.
- **Sequential Filter Session-based kNN (SF-SKNN)** [17]: This method uses a modified scoring function, but in a more restrictive way. Given the last event and a related item of the current session, only items for recommendation that appeared directly after the item in the training data at least once are considered.
- **GRU4REC** [14]: This method models user sessions with the help of an RNN with Gated Recurrent Units (GRU) in order to predict the probability of the subsequent item clicks given the beginning of a session. The standard GRU layer keeps track of a hidden state that encodes the previously occurring items in the same session.
- **Factorized Personalized Markov Chains (FPMC)** [30]: This method combines MC and traditional user-item matrix factorization in a three dimensional tensor factorization approach. The third dimension captures the transition probabilities from one item to another. Canonical Tensor Decomposition

is used to factor the cube into latent matrices, which can then be used to predict a ranking.

- **Factored Item Similarity Models (FISM)** [18]: This method is based on item-item factorization but does not incorporate sequential item-to-item transitions. For user and item, a score is calculated as the sum of latent vector products between the item and the items already rated by the user. Bayesian Personalized Ranking pairwise loss function is used to optimize the top-n recommendations.
- **Factorized Sequential Prediction with Item Similarity Models (FOSSIL)** [13]: This method combines FISM with factorized Markov chains to incorporate sequential information into the model. Using a weighted sum with a global factor and a personalized factor, the model extends FISM by a factorized MC to capture the sequential dynamics. Bayesian Personalized Ranking is used as the loss function to rank suitable items over negative examples.
- **Session-based Matrix Factorization (SMF)** [24]: In this method, the score for a session with the most recent item and other items is computed as a weighted combination of session preferences and sequential dynamics. The embedded session latent vector for the current session is multiplied with an item latent vector for item to compute a relevance score for the item regarding the current session.

Metrics. The following metrics were used.

- **Mean Reciprocal Rank (MRR):** is measure to evaluate methods that return a ranked list of responses to queries (Q). It is calculated as:

$$MRR = \frac{1}{Q} \sum_{j=1}^{Q} \frac{1}{rank_j} \qquad (10)$$

Table 2. Hit rate (HR), Mean Reciprocal Rank (MRR) and item coverage (COV) results for list lengths of 20 and 10 on the RCS15 dataset .

Algorithm	MRR@20	HR@20	COV@20	MRR@10	HR@10	COV@10
GRU4REC	0.308	0.683	0.504	0.301	0.591	0.431
SR	0.304	0.653	0.668	0.298	0.569	0.592
SMF	0.302	0.666	0.565	0.295	0.575	0.486
MC	0.300	0.642	0.645	0.295	0.562	0.584
AR	0.289	0.636	0.630	0.283	0.550	0.548
V-SKNN	0.283	0.653	0.619	0.277	0.563	0.534
S-SKNN	0.272	0.602	0.655	0.267	0.531	0.543
SF-SKNN	0.270	0.589	0.619	0.266	0.524	0.545
S-KNN	0.266	0.621	0.634	0.259	0.526	0.520
IKNN	0.208	0.486	0.755	0.203	0.408	0.671
FPMC	0.201	0.363	0.975	0.198	0.311	0.908
BPR-MF	0.176	0.235	0.911	0.175	0.223	0.793
FISM	0.115	0.162	0.974	0.114	0.149	0.917
FOSSIL	0.062	0.190	0.917	0.058	0.135	0.806
COV-Greedy	0.303	0.673	0.758	0.295	0.576	0.672

Table 3. Hit rate (HR), Mean Reciprocal Rank (MRR) and item coverage (COV) results for list lengths of 20 and 10 on the TMALL dataset .

Algorithm	MRR@20	HR@20	COV@20	MRR@10	HR@10	COV@10
GRU4REC	0.129	0.277	0.151	0.125	0.225	0.109
SR	0.128	0.242	0.569	0.125	0.206	0.421
SMF	0.121	0.261	0.261	0.118	0.213	0.193
MC	0.116	0.200	0.498	0.114	0.178	0.391
AR	0.129	0.262	0.509	0.126	0.217	0.358
V-SKNN	0.179	0.373	0.464	0.175	0.312	0.320
S-SKNN	0.185	0.387	0.467	0.181	0.330	0.309
SF-SKNN	0.136	0.216	0.436	0.135	0.203	0.338
S-KNN	0.182	0.404	0.381	0.177	0.334	0.249
IKNN	0.051	0.150	0.728	0.048	0.112	0.575
FPMC	0.101	0.119	0.880	0.100	0.114	0.730
BPR-MF	0.159	0.204	0.723	0.159	0.197	0.534
FISM	0.024	0.037	0.752	0.023	0.032	0.586
FOSSIL	0.001	0.004	0.598	0.001	0.003	0.457
COV-Greedy	0.174	0.365	0.757	0.170	0.253	0.463

- **Hit Rate (HR):** is the ratio of the number of user interactions, i to the length l of a list of ranked items impressed upon the user. Hit Rate is calculated as:

$$HR = \frac{i}{l}, \tag{11}$$

where $0 \leq i \leq l$

- **Coverage (COV):** is the fraction of items in the training data the model is able to recommend on a test set. We denote the possible recommendations that an implemented recommendation algorithm can produce as I_{rec} and the total number of items as I_{total}. Coverage is calculated as:

$$COV = \frac{I_{rec}}{I_{total}} \tag{12}$$

Results and Discussion. Tables 2, 3 and 4 show the Hit rate (HR), Mean Reciprocal Rank (MRR) and item coverage (COV) results for list lengths of 20 and 10 on the RCS15, TMALL and RETAILR datasets respectively. The lowest accuracy values are almost consistently achieved across all datasets by the family of Factorized Markov Chain approaches (FISM, FPMC and FOSSIL) and the session-aware BPR-MF variant. What we observe if that our COV-Greedy approach performs consistently well by being in the top five performing models across all datasets.

Table 4. Hit rate (HR), Mean Reciprocal Rank (MRR) and item coverage (COV) results for list lengths of 20 and 10 on the RETAILR dataset .

Algorithm	MRR@20	HR@20	COV@20	MRR@10	HR@10	COV@10
GRU4REC	0.243	0.480	0.602	0.238	0.415	0.478
SR	0.245	0.419	0.524	0.243	0.386	0.458
SMF	0.225	0.459	0.449	0.221	0.393	0.360
MC	0.230	0.359	0.411	0.228	0.343	0.383
AR	0.241	0.439	0.544	0.238	0.390	0.449
V-SKNN	0.338	0.573	0.575	0.334	0.519	0.474
S-SKNN	0.337	0.583	0.566	0.333	0.528	0.445
SF-SKNN	0.260	0.358	0.403	0.259	0.350	0.373
S-KNN	0.337	0.583	0.566	0.333	0.528	0.445
IKNN	0.107	0.240	0.584	0.105	0.202	0.505
FPMC	0.273	0.320	0.929	0.272	0.309	0.777
BPR-MF	0.303	0.357	0.824	0.303	0.352	0.627
FISM	0.075	0.132	0.848	0.074	0.112	0.672
FOSSIL	0.022	0.058	0.753	0.020	0.043	0.560
COV-Greedy	0.318	0.579	0.761	0.307	0.520	0.631

The simple pairwise association methods AR and SR mostly occupy the middle positions in the model performance comparison. GRU4REC is consistently among the top five algorithms in this comparison in terms of the hit rate and exhibits competitive performance results also with respect to the MRR. For each of the datasets, one of the proposed neighborhood-based methods was usually the winner in terms of the hit rate and the MRR. The most consistent performance of the neighborhood-based methods is achieved with the V-SKNN method which uses a specific sequence-aware similarity measure that gives more weight to the most recent interactions.

Table 5 shows the average of Hit rate (HR), Mean Reciprocal Rank (MRR) and item coverage (COV) results for a list length of 20 on all datasets. The observation here is that on the average, across all datasets, COV-Greedy is the best performing model for HR and joint second best performing model with S-SKNN on MRR. In terms of COV, the best performing models were the factorization models which did poorly on the accuracy metrics. However, COV-Greedy was able to obtain a high item coverage by placing third for this quality metric.

Table 5. Average of Hit rate (HR), Mean Reciprocal Rank (MRR) and item coverage (COV) results for a list length of 20 on all datasets. The best performing models are in bold font and the second highest ones are underlined.

Algorithm	MRR	HR	COV
GRU4REC	0.227	0.480	0.419
SR	0.226	0.438	0.587
SMF	0.216	0.462	0.425
MC	0.215	0.400	0.518
AR	0.220	0.446	0.561
V-SKNN	**0.267**	<u>0.533</u>	0.553
S-SKNN	<u>0.265</u>	0.524	0.563
SF-SKNN	0.222	0.388	0.486
S-KNN	0.262	0.536	0.527
IKNN	0.122	0.292	0.689
FPMC	0.192	0.267	0.669
BPR-MF	0.213	0.265	<u>0.819</u>
FISM	0.071	0.110	**0.858**
FOSSIL	0.028	0.084	0.756
COV-Greedy	<u>0.265</u>	**0.539**	0.759

6 Conclusion

In this work, we have proposed a two-stage approach to carry out session-based recommendations. We specifically focus on the quality of the recommendation system by boosting item coverage while maintaining a good recommendation accuracy relative to state-of-the-art methods. To rank our candidates for the next event prediction task, we pre-trained a BERT language model using session sequences as sentences. We then trained a skip-gram model with negative sampling to generate candidate items that co-occur with a given query set. The query set allowed us to mitigate the effects of an accidental click if any had occurred.

Next, we use a multi-armed bandit epsilon-greedy approach to boost recommendation coverage by balancing the exploration-exploitation trade-off between selecting candidates solely from the skip-gram model or augmenting with items that weakly co-occur with other items from a coverage map. Experiments with the e-commerce datasets revealed that, without sacrificing coverage, our proposed COV-Greedy model's performance is comparable to the strongest state-of-the-art baselines on the session-based recommendation task.

References

1. Anarfi, R., Kwapong, B., Fletcher, K.K.: Towards a reinforcement learning-based exploratory search for mashup tag recommendation. In: 2021 IEEE International Conference on Smart Data Services (SMDS), pp. 8–17. IEEE (2021)
2. Anarfi, R., Fletcher, K.K.: A reinforcement learning approach to web API recommendation for mashup development. In: 2019 IEEE World Congress on Services (SERVICES), vol. 2642, pp. 372–373. IEEE (2019)
3. Anarfi, R., Kwapong, B., Fletcher, K.K.: Desc2tag: a reinforcement learning approach to mashup tag recommendation. In: 2020 IEEE International Conference on Services Computing (SCC), pp. 475–477. IEEE (2020)
4. Chamberlain, B.P., Rossi, E., Shiebler, D., Sedhain, S., Bronstein, M.M.: Tuning word2vec for large scale recommendation systems. In: Fourteenth ACM Conference on Recommender Systems, pp. 732–737 (2020)
5. Devlin, J., Chang, M.W., Lee, K., Toutanova, K.: BERT: pre-training of deep bidirectional transformers for language understanding. arXiv preprint arXiv:1810.04805 (2018)
6. Esmeli, R., Bader-El-Den, M., Abdullahi, H.: Using word2vec recommendation for improved purchase prediction. In: 2020 International Joint Conference on Neural Networks (IJCNN), pp. 1–8. IEEE (2020)
7. Felício, C.Z., Paixão, K.V., Barcelos, C.A., Preux, P.: A multi-armed bandit model selection for cold-start user recommendation. In: Proceedings of the 25th Conference on User Modeling, Adaptation and Personalization, pp. 32–40 (2017)
8. Fletcher, K.K.: A method for dealing with data sparsity and cold-start limitations in service recommendation using personalized preferences. In: 2017 IEEE International Conference on Cognitive Computing (ICCC), pp. 72–79. IEEE (2017)
9. Ge, M., Delgado-Battenfeld, C., Jannach, D.: Beyond accuracy: evaluating recommender systems by coverage and serendipity. In: Proceedings of the Fourth ACM Conference on Recommender Systems, pp. 257–260 (2010)
10. Gimelfarb, M., Sanner, S., Lee, C.G.: ϵ-bmc: a Bayesian ensemble approach to epsilon-greedy exploration in model-free reinforcement learning. arXiv preprint arXiv:2007.00869 (2020)
11. Greenstein-Messica, A., Rokach, L., Friedman, M.: Session-based recommendations using item embedding. In: Proceedings of the 22nd International Conference on Intelligent User Interfaces, pp. 629–633 (2017)
12. Gunawardana, A., Shani, G.: A survey of accuracy evaluation metrics of recommendation tasks. J. Mach. Learn. Res. **10**(12) (2009)
13. He, R., McAuley, J.: Fusing similarity models with Markov chains for sparse sequential recommendation. In: 2016 IEEE 16th International Conference on Data Mining (ICDM), pp. 191–200. IEEE (2016)
14. Hidasi, B., Karatzoglou, A.: Recurrent neural networks with top-k gains for session-based recommendations. In: Proceedings of the 27th ACM International Conference on Information and Knowledge Management, pp. 843–852 (2018)
15. Hidasi, B., Karatzoglou, A., Baltrunas, L., Tikk, D.: Session-based recommendations with recurrent neural networks. arXiv preprint arXiv:1511.06939 (2015)
16. Intayoad, W., Kamyod, C., Temdee, P.: Reinforcement learning based on contextual bandits for personalized online learning recommendation systems. Wirel. Pers. Commun. 1–16 (2020)
17. Jannach, D., Ludewig, M.: When recurrent neural networks meet the neighborhood for session-based recommendation. In: Proceedings of the Eleventh ACM Conference on Recommender Systems, pp. 306–310 (2017)

18. Kabbur, S., Ning, X., Karypis, G.: Fism: factored item similarity models for top-n recommender systems. In: Proceedings of the 19th ACM SIGKDD International Conference on Knowledge Discovery and Data Mining, pp. 659–667 (2013)
19. Kamehkhosh, I., Jannach, D., Ludewig, M.: A comparison of frequent pattern techniques and a deep learning method for session-based recommendation. In: RecTemp@ RecSys, pp. 50–56 (2017)
20. Kaminskas, M., Bridge, D.: Diversity, serendipity, novelty, and coverage: a survey and empirical analysis of beyond-accuracy objectives in recommender systems. ACM Trans. Interact. Intell. Sys. (TiiS) **7**(1), 1–42 (2016)
21. Kawamae, N.: Serendipitous recommendations via innovators. In: Proceedings of the 33rd International ACM SIGIR Conference on Research and Development in Information Retrieval, pp. 218–225 (2010)
22. Kwapong, B.A., Anarfi, R., Fletcher, K.K.: Personalized service recommendation based on user dynamic preferences. In: Ferreira, J.E., Musaev, A., Zhang, L.-J. (eds.) SCC 2019. LNCS, vol. 11515, pp. 77–91. Springer, Cham (2019). https://doi.org/10.1007/978-3-030-23554-3_6
23. Kwapong, B.A., Anarfi, R., Fletcher, K.K.: Collaborative learning using LSTM-RNN for personalized recommendation. In: Wang, Q., Xia, Y., Seshadri, S., Zhang, L.-J. (eds.) SCC 2020. LNCS, vol. 12409, pp. 35–49. Springer, Cham (2020). https://doi.org/10.1007/978-3-030-59592-0_3
24. Ludewig, M., Jannach, D.: Evaluation of session-based recommendation algorithms. User Model. User-Adapt. Inter. **28**(4), 331–390 (2018)
25. Ludewig, M., Mauro, N., Latifi, S., Jannach, D.: Empirical analysis of session-based recommendation algorithms. User Model. User-Adapt. Inter. **31**(1), 149–181 (2021)
26. Maccatrozzo, V., Terstall, M., Aroyo, L., Schreiber, G.: SIRUP: serendipity in recommendations via user perceptions. In: Proceedings of the 22nd International Conference on Intelligent User Interfaces, pp. 35–44 (2017)
27. Mikolov, T., Sutskever, I., Chen, K., Corrado, G.S., Dean, J.: Distributed representations of words and phrases and their compositionality. In: Advances in Neural Information Processing Systems, pp. 3111–3119 (2013)
28. Norris, J.R., Norris, J.R.: Markov Chains, No. 2. Cambridge University Press (1998)
29. Rendle, S., Freudenthaler, C., Gantner, Z., Schmidt-Thieme, L.: BPR: bayesian personalized ranking from implicit feedback. arXiv preprint arXiv:1205.2618 (2012)
30. Rendle, S., Freudenthaler, C., Schmidt-Thieme, L.: Factorizing personalized Markov chains for next-basket recommendation. In: Proceedings of the 19th International Conference on World Wide Web, pp. 811–820 (2010)
31. Sanz-Cruzado, J., Castells, P., López, E.: A simple multi-armed nearest-neighbor bandit for interactive recommendation. In: Proceedings of the 13th ACM Conference on Recommender Systems, pp. 358–362 (2019)
32. Shani, G., Gunawardana, A.: Evaluating recommendation systems. In: Ricci, F., Rokach, L., Shapira, B., Kantor, P.B. (eds.) Recommender Systems Handbook, pp. 257–297. Springer, Boston, MA (2011). https://doi.org/10.1007/978-0-387-85820-3_8
33. Sun, F., et al.: BERT4rec: sequential recommendation with bidirectional encoder representations from transformer. In: Proceedings of the 28th ACM International Conference on Information and Knowledge Management, pp. 1441–1450 (2019)
34. Sutton, R.S., Barto, A.G.: Reinforcement Learning: An Introduction. MIT Press, Cambridge (2018)

35. Tan, Y.K., Xu, X., Liu, Y.: Improved recurrent neural networks for session-based recommendations. In: Proceedings of the 1st Workshop on Deep Learning for Recommender Systems, pp. 17–22 (2016)
36. Vaswani, A., et al.: Attention is all you need. arXiv preprint arXiv:1706.03762 (2017)
37. Wu, S., Tang, Y., Zhu, Y., Wang, L., Xie, X., Tan, T.: Session-based recommendation with graph neural networks. In: Proceedings of the AAAI Conference on Artificial Intelligence, vol. 33, pp. 346–353 (2019)
38. Xu, Y., et al.: Neural serendipity recommendation: exploring the balance between accuracy and novelty with sparse explicit feedback. ACM Trans. Knowl. Discov. from Data (TKDD) **14**(4), 1–25 (2020)
39. Zeng, C., Wang, Q., Mokhtari, S., Li, T.: Online context-aware recommendation with time varying multi-armed bandit. In: Proceedings of the 22nd ACM SIGKDD International Conference on Knowledge Discovery and Data Mining, pp. 2025–2034 (2016)
40. Zuva, K., Zuva, T.: Diversity and serendipity in recommender systems. In: Proceedings of the International Conference on Big Data and Internet of Thing, pp. 120–124 (2017)

The Second-Person Standpoint and Moral Machine

Hanlin Ma(✉) (iD)

Suzhou University of Science and Technology, Suzhou, China
fanfan2011cn2000@gmail.com

Abstract. Given the need for Human-Machine moral Interaction, an AI system that focuses on moral theory involving intersubjectivity is worthy of attention. We will build a network knowledge representation framework based on the second-person standpoint moral theory to analyze the design philosophy of a *general artificial intelligence* (AGI) moral machine. We then use this framework to investigate an interactive moral machine designed by Bello and Bringsjord (2013). In constructing a feature of mindreading, their study faces philosophical challenges to combine the empirical source configuration of its inheritance function and the multi-world setting of the *Polyscheme* itself. We try to prove that the integrated structure of the Polyscheme based on a third-person perspective, multi-world setting cannot afford a continuous self that can accommodate enough diversity of the stimulation relationship between the concept of self and other. Moreover, we suggest that the psychological distance structure of mindreading should mainly come from the internal "self" of the system. This requires the system to have an intrinsic kernel, meaning a design philosophy completely different from the integrated style of Polyscheme.

Keywords: Second-person standpoint · Moral machine · Artificial general intelligence · Human-machine interaction · AI system · Mindreading

1 Introduction

With the improvement of research and application, the participation of AI in society is expected to increase significantly, and AI will increasingly enter into moral interactions. Therefore, researchers have steadily become concerned about how to make "machines" have ethical attributes. There are two types of moral machines. One functions only as an instrument for the moral enhancement of humans, while the other is a moral thinking machine with moral subjectivity. The former is a kind of specialized artificial intelligence technology designed to help humans obtain morally sound cognition, make moral decisions, comply with moral norms, and so on (Savulescu and Maslen 2015). Comprehensively introduced by Wendell Wallach and Colin Allen (2008), specialized AI is exemplified by Medical Ethics Expert (MedEthEx) designed by Michael Anderson and others (Anderson et al. 2006), the Truth-Teller by McLaren and Ashley (1995), and Marcello Guarini's Ethical Case Classifier (the Moral Case Classifier, MCC in short)

(Guarini 2011). The latter type of system is hoped to simultaneously realize the full range of human cognitive abilities and human-like moral attributes. For example, Wallach and Allen once collaborated with Stan Franklin, the creator of the LIDA (Learning Intelligent Distribution Agent) system, to explore how to implement a universal moral decision model relying on LIDA's high-level cognitive framework (Wallach et al. 2010).

Moral machine scientists have their preferences for the mastery and application of moral theories. They focus on either specific applied ethical content (such as what MedEthEx does) or the normative properties of ethical norms itself (such as what MCC does). Others may be concerned with moral decision-making issues, referring to how to make moral systems emerge for particular collectives from systems representing conflicting moral imperatives (Dameski 2018). At present, it seems that only a few researchers consider AI moral systems from the perspective of inter-subject interactions. Therefore, moral-philosophical theories involving intersubjectivity are rarely utilized to assist in designing or evaluating a moral system. The second-person standpoint moral philosophy is dedicated to constructing moral knowledge that endorses intersubjectivity. It emphasizes decentralization, indeterminacy, and so forth. Influential ethical theories in the twentieth century, such as moral constructivism (Rawls 1980), virtue ethics (Williams 2008), and the ethics of care (Gilligan 1993) have potential connections with this theory. P. F. Strawson (2014), Stephen Darwall (2006), and R. Jay Wallace (2019) hold the most influential second-person theories of morality. Their central idea is that moral knowledge is modified in human interactions in the light of each other's reactions. Moral knowledge neither comes from the independent realm of the third-person nor is it purely the subjective construction of a first-person, but is determined by a multi-distributed network process. When building a second-person moral AGI system, we must thus consider how to establish a self-knowledge representation and control system compatible with these presuppositions and further establish a mindreading representation system involving intersubjectivity. From the standpoint of adopted design elements, the design philosophy of the specialized moral machine (SMM), the individual moral thinking machine (IMM), and the second-person moral thinking machine (S-pMM) can be compared through the following graph (Fig. 1).

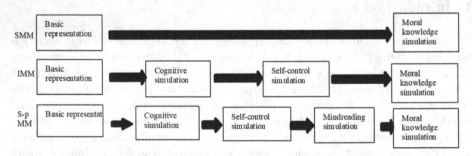

Fig. 1. Arrow indicates designing based on the former item

So far, only the work of Paul Bello and Selmer Bringsjord (2013) has involved the moral thinking machine construction from an intersubjective perspective. Their AGI model Polyscheme is one of the pioneers in the realm. Although the framework of

Polyscheme they used has gradually declined, the traits of its design philosophy are still very representative, such as LIDA and OpenCog, which are still active in the same way as "integrating approach". Because of the framework's integrated basic structure and its reliance on possible-world semantics, its self-knowledge model will be faced with some difficulties, which blends with the problem encountered by Bello and Bringsjord when using a third-person criterion of inheritance function to construct intersubjectivity. The paper is organized as follows. In Sect. 2, we present a second-person concept cycle network to analyze what the cognitive states should ascribe to. This network is joined by a *monotonic inheritance relationship*, which does not provide a *third-person* perspective to the computing process. In Sect. 3, we introduce how Bello and Bringsjord characterize Knobe and Nichols's measurement of *causality involving self*, based on construal level theory (CLT). Next, in Sect. 4, we will show that a central control of Polyscheme actually takes charge of the integrated box of possible worlds. In Sect. 5, we find that this kind of *integrated* AGI system cannot build a self with continuous history, and cannot represent all the significant similarity between different possible worlds, which means different *selves*. In Sect. 6, we introduce another AGI system (NARS) that may more closely match the second-person concept cycle network, and explain why this is so.

2 Second-Person Concept Cycle Network and Intersubjectivity

Stephen Darwall systematically uses the second-person standpoint to study the issue of normative origin. In a nutshell, the *second-person cycle* he proposed refers to the fact that the subject and others in a sense share a way of *explaining* each other's behavior (*second-person reasoning*) and a way of *requiring* and *blaming* each other (requirement and accountability). This shared basis is called second-person authority, and all these concepts are mutually defined. For example, there is a connection between *requirement* and *accountability*, because people generally believe that moral *requirements* are based on *accountability* or *obligation*—if you don't do something you are supposed do, it means you fail to meet the requirements. Under the second-person theoretical presupposition, accountability is also in line with requirement, because the structure of accountability is based on Strawson's *"reactive attitude"*. That is to say, I have to comply with certain responsibilities precisely because others have a reactive attitude toward me. If I step on someone else's feet, she/he will express resentment against me, which can be understood as expressing some kind of moral requirement and moral authority. It is based on this attitude that I establish the viewpoint of not stepping on others' feet. However, for a rational responsibility construction process, we have to look at the "reason" behind the attitude of others, which in turn is related to responsibility, because she/he will feel that you are responsible for this attitude. All of the above is connected to "second-person authority"—all people in the relationship believe that everyone recognizes the legitimacy of each other's reaction and attitude.

Formally speaking, the definition of the second-person normative concept is distributed, which means that no concept in the circle can be defined as an atom, thus determining the connotation and extension of other concepts. Therefore, we recommend using multiple inheritance relationships to describe this normativity. For example, the semantics of shared accountability by others and me can be inherited by the meaning of his requirement of me (which I'm also certain of), which is "you have to do it" (to be responsible to him); it is also inherited by reasons for others to condemn me morally (which I also agree with) to some extent; it is inherited by the second-person authority shared by my Self and others' Selves.

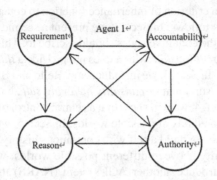

Fig. 2. Solid line indicates monotone inheritance

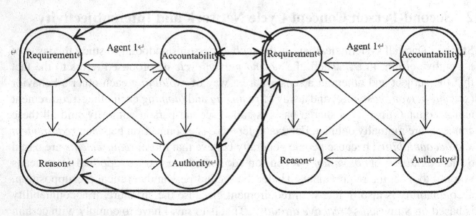

Fig. 3. Schematic diagram of a conceptual network between two agents in an ideal situation

For Darwall, it is also feasible to describe these concepts using inheritance relationships in other directions under ideal circumstances. From the perspective of knowledge representation, it is thus merely necessary to construct a model concerning one of the concepts, with the other three being partially represented. In an idealized situation, this is not a typical *inheritance logic*, because inheritance relationships are generally asymmetric (Al-Asady 1995). If the relationship between subjects is not involved, it can be assumed that the representation of the moral concept network is as shown in Fig. 2. For example, the definition of the "reason" is determined by the relationship between it and other concepts. It is not difficult to implement a network alone. For instance, an artificial neural network (ANN) can theoretically meet the needs of this data structure. Apart from the distributed definition, the second-person perspective also requires the conceptual loop network to be characterized by a reactive attitude, namely the subject's judgment of other subjects' experiences. Here, a representation framework involving the subject (or the Self) is needed. How to design this framework and combine it with specific distributed technology paths will be the core task of building S-pMM.

The biggest challenge here is the contradiction between the moral knowledge representation and the computing knowledge representation. Darwall's *Kantian* tendency presupposed substantial completeness of his moral knowledge representation, which perceived norms as a *monotonic inheritance relationship* (Fig. 2). Supposing we have acquired a self-representation framework for knowledge in some way and stayed with this framework, it is impossible for the machine to halt in the process of characterizing the second-person normative knowledge. As the representation of self-knowledge is first-person, the iterative subjective perspectives will explode in combination when some people assume that others' subjective perspectives are not equal to theirs. Take the rule "don't do to others what you don't want done to yourself" as an example. From the second-person perspective, this sentence can be reduced to the conjunction of the following two sentences: A = "We are unwilling to be the cause of situations we do not want to see" and B = "In our eyes, we share this causal mechanism with others". Consequently, this rule has become a normative law, and it is also a moral requirement for myself, which naturally has moral authority. Furthermore, B can be reduced to the conjunction of the following three sentences: C = "Others are in our eyes reluctant to be the cause of the situation we do not want to see"; D = "In the eyes of us and others, we are loath to be the cause of conditions we do not want to see", and E = "In our opinion, we share with others the causal explanation after the first 'in our eyes' in D". Besides, E can be reduced to "F∧G∧H∧I...". In a sense, we can equate this nesting situation with the infinite expansion of *reflexive transitive closures*.

Assuming that public knowledge is a closed first-person *iterative combination* (which means a complete second-person standpoint), the amount of information in the *reflexive transitive closure* of a relationship tends to be infinite in the absence of any public knowledge (suppose moral knowledge is a networked structure). This problem is similar to the *mud baby puzzle*: if the father does not give any public knowledge, the two babies will never find out whether they have mud on their foreheads. There are two schemes to solve this problem: (1) Abandon the self-knowledge representation framework and interpret the above nesting situation as synonymous repetition; (2) Abandon completeness and consider the breaking of the cycle as the subject's incompleteness belief. Although scheme 1 retains the second-person cycle, its knowledge representation framework is third-person. Scheme 2 retains the second person to a certain extent, but breaks the cycle and also gives up completeness. However, as experience evolves, normative content can evolve under an open first-person knowledge framework. If taking the scheme 1, we will face two issues. First, distributed morality will lose its significance because the tension between different definitions no longer exists. Second, Darwall's practice of classifying some abnormal normative behaviors as third-person perspectives will no longer be of any ethical or distinguishable representational significance. The "Self-conceit" phenomenon specifically labeled by him refers to the phenomenon of equating self-perspective norms with objective norms. In his view, his own will is the source of norms, namely the premise of egoistic ethical egoism (Darwall 2006, 136). Therefore, we recommend scheme 2, signifying that we must use a certain Defeasible Inheritance network with a non-monotonic reasoning mechanism. The requirements of system 1 are as follows: The inheritance network is a directed acyclic graph; the uncertainty of the inheritance relationship can be determined by some kind of "inherited truth function". Assuming that the inherited truth function is f(x), the conceptual inheritance diagram of the dual agent is shown in Fig. 4 (the figure merely presents one truth function).

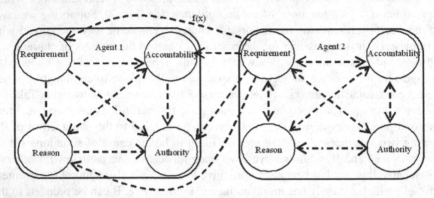

Fig. 4. Schematic diagram of the conceptual network between two agents, with the dashed lines indicating incomplete inheritance

3   Psychological Distance and Construal Level Theory

After establishing a fundamental conceptual inheritance relationship framework between subjects, the next step is to establish empirical quantification of the characterization for *inheriting functions*. This system could be set up in many ways, depending on different cognitive science achievements. However, considering the issue of adaptability, it is currently suggested to place this function under the framework of the mindreading theory. According to Bello and Bringsjord's theory (2012), disparate psychological distances can be analyzed qualitatively or quantitatively through the interpretation of construal level theory (CLT). Based on Knobe and Nichols's measurement of "causality involving self" (Knobe and Nichols 2011), a correlation analysis between different forms of causality is established in line with different types of self and the richness of cognitive content. Bello and Bringsjord suggested using CLT for reinterpretation in the light of their data, directly deeming different types of causality as different levels of abstraction. Hence, a correlation between the length of the causal chain and data that represent selves is established.

Originally proposed by Trope and Liberman (2010), CLT is a widely proven theory, asserting that similar people will have dissimilar cognitions of an identical event under different *psychological distances*, which is reflected in different construal levels of the event. The recognition of events with a longer psychological distance is more abstract and essential (which means a high construal level); the recognition of events with a shorter psychological distance is more specific and direct (which means a low construal level). The characteristic of psychological distance is not fixed, although mainstream items are time (close or not), space (close or not), the closeness of social relationships, and real or counterfactual events. Under the right conditions, the relationship between psychological distance and the construal level is symmetric. In other words, we can infer the construal level through psychological distance, and vice versa. Moreover, psychological distance is the "distance" between an event and the "self". Since the "self" is an abstract and complex concept, the "distance" from it may have many dimensions. Knobe and Nichols divide the concept of the "self" into three categories: the physical concept of the self, the psychological concept of the self, and the executive concept of the self. The psychological concept of the self refers to the mental process in the sense of psychology or cognitive science, which is the kind of "mental events" that philosopher Donald Davidson (2001) or Jaegwon Kim (1973) worked on. The corresponding causal relationship is *mental causation*. The concept of self-implementation refers to an "agent", a similar "subject" commonly used in the history of philosophy, and its metaphysical properties are not limited by physical time and causality (in contrast to from the psychological concept of the self). The corresponding causal relationship is *agent causation* (Clarke 1993; O'Connor 1996).

To find out which causal relationship is more easily used by people at different psychological distances, Knobe and Nichols tried to analyze target events through questionnaires. Once causation involving the "self" is associated with psychological distance, we can use this as a basis to establish a psychological distance between individuals. When the target event happens to someone else, the causal judgment we make is about the relationship between "the self of the other person and the event". Then, causal judgments about ourselves and different others can be made—listed as an extension of inherited functions. The detail is as follows: When zooming out and examining a person's behavior in a broader context, people are apt to view emotions or the body as part of the self. At this time, people are not explicit about the concept of the self, and are inclined to use the concept of the "executive self" to explain behavior in an abstract and unified way. When zooming in and examining a person's behavior in a more specific situation, people are likely to distinguish the concept of the self in a relatively clear way, such as not considering emotion as the "self" part. When the psychological process is separated from the "executing self", a psychological process rather than the agent (a "thin" self) may be regarded as the cause of the behavior (Knobe and Nichols 2011). Strictly speaking, the *uncertainty* concerning the causal attribution of the self regarding others' behavior can be perceived as the *extension* of the inheritance function.

Nevertheless, Bello and Bringsjord have another plan. They use the length of the causal chain to represent different psychological distances and use the level of abstraction to explain why humans have different causality under various psychological distances. This plan may lead to the immaturity of the mindreading representation. According to CLT, a higher level of interpretation means more abstract, vague, and inaccurate features, which is an economic thinking principle. A series of actions are taken as: "I want to eat sandwiches, I intend to make them. After opening the refrigerator, I take out various materials to make sandwiches, and later a sandwich appears on the table". When attributing this behavior, I tend to use the distal "I" as the reason for "a sandwich appeared on the table", for we don't have time to cope with so many reasons. In this way, the distal cause can easily be wrapped in an "agent". However, in cases where the psychological distance is shorter, the subject has sufficient resources to analyze the proximal situation, which explains the lower construal level of the relationship. For example, more people will tend to think that the reason for "the refrigerator is opened" is "I want to eat sandwiches" rather than "I" when the previous case is changed into "As I want to eat sandwiches, I intend to make them, and the refrigerator is opened".

Please note that the so-called "I" here does not mean the "first-person" as defined in Sect. 2 but a specific instance of knowledge representation. From a philosophical point of view, this is a configuration of knowledge content based on "de se". There are many theories on this issue, and Bello and Bringsjord may pay more attention to Neil Feit's theory (Feit 2008). Feit tried to defend David Lewis's content-property theory, claiming that all psychological content is property, not a proposition. That means that all material of this statement is merely supervenient on the actual physical cause and effect. In "my first-person standpoint", the psychological content of others is characterized by counterfactual statements of my psychological content. When considering what others think, we often "simulate" others' thoughts as "if I were him, I would do Φ" on which the assumptions of "I" for others' thoughts are built. My counterfactual cognitive content will be different form "his" in "my first-person standpoint". The difference can be precisely described by psychological distance. In this sense, some hypothetical functions can be recursively produced based on research data like that of Knobe and Nichols to describe the quantitative relationship between psychological distance (causal chain length) and different simulation content. Furthermore, many specialized learning algorithms can be applied here. In summary, if the above model is used to construct intersubjectivity, the function used to describe this property is based on the environment. In other words, it has no direct relationship with the subject's internal history or various intricate internal cognitive properties.

4   The Knowledge Representation of Mindreading Under the Framework of Polyscheme

The artificial intelligence framework used by Bello and Bringsjord is derived from the Polyscheme system built by Nicholas L. Cassimatis, who strove to build an "integrated" AGI system, referring to the integration of different specialist subsystems into a unified system with general capabilities. Given that different specialists can normally deal with a particular type of work or one or a few aspects of an event, we can understand an aspect as only dealing with a specific property of an event. The purpose of Polyscheme is to combine different property processing capabilities so that the machine can handle complex and multifaceted events like a human—a comprehensive property processor. The system presents a "foci" state, which is a proposition that can be used to connect all specialists. For the sake of the synergy between different specialists, Cassimatis set up many protocols, thereby ensuring that "all specialists focus on the same proposition at the same time". In line with a "de se" representation, Polyscheme may presuppose incomplete semantics, signifying that some contents in this world are propositions or can at least be represented by propositions. Besides, it also means an objective representation. As we will see later, this allows the self-knowledge representation that is constructed in

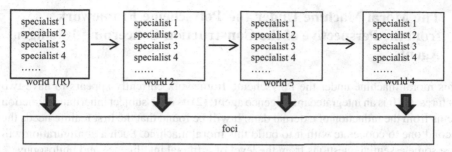

Fig. 5. The dashed line indicates the inheritance relationship between possible worlds, with the down arrow pointing to the proposition

the Polyscheme system to have some properties that do not meet our expectations in the second-person analysis.

The foci proposition is the kernel of the specialist net and includes four elements: a predicate, zero to multiple arguments about the predicate, the interval tense, and possible-world semantics. The last element can be used to settle the entire range of counterfactual problems, uncertainty problems, and "other mind" problems called the "mindreading" problem (Cassimatis 2001). The R world is the real world defined by Polyscheme, and other worlds are a subset or a superset of R. What is the target world "?W" can be characterized as more false or real (the relevant framework is shown in Fig. 5). When all the ?W is inherited to R, there are two sorts of inheritance relationships. One is hard inheritance, with the symbol "==>", analogous to modal necessity. Suppose E designates the temporal interval representing "at all times", then the reasoning "If John is happy, he is Full". is written as "Happy (john, E, R) ==> Full (john, E, R)". The other is soft inheritance, with the symbol expressed as "(cost)>". The value of cost ranges from 0 to 1. Generally, it is expressed as: Happy (john, E, R) (.80)> Full (john, E, R), and the justification of this reasoning is a problem of degree (80 is a default value). Weak inheritance is employed to help crudely describe the psychological distance and causal chain length related to mindreading. Treating different agents as disparate worlds, we then get the following representation of the inheritance relationship concerning relational predicates in the eyes of different subjects at any moment (Let ?Relation be any relationship, here it can be causal relationship; ?e1 is any entity, and t1 is any time):

?Relation(e1;?t; R)∧IsCounterfactualWorld(?w, E, R) (cost) >?Relation (e1;?t;?w) (Bello and Bringsjord 2012).

The setting of cost is: the larger the value, the closer the counterfactual world of the mindreading object is to the real world (that means from the first-person perspective). The value is related to the length of the causal chain. The specific constraint judgment threshold is given by the external CLT data. Although this is not sufficient to serve for the composition and reasoning of the second-person distributed knowledge structure we mentioned, it may be hoped to build a basis for it. At least, the aforementioned inheritance relationship can assist the subject in recognizing the distance between the moral reason of others and his own. Hence, the similarities and differences between his own responsibility view and that of mindreading can be evaluated.

5   The Moral Machine Under the Polyscheme Framework from the Perspective of the Construction Concerning Intelligent Agents

This moral machine under the Polyscheme framework currently appears to have two features: (1) It is an integrated intelligence agent; (2) its inter-subject inheritance function stems from the induction of external data. It will be found that the first feature needs the second one to cooperate with it to build this moral machine. Such a configuration will face some essential questions from the level of artificial intelligence and philosophy.

As we see, the mindreading representation of Polyscheme is counterfactual reasoning, which involves relationships between different worlds. The worlds here refer to the agreements reached by all specialists concerning representations of the same foci proposition. Cassimatis's construction of cognitive subjects is based on Baars's theory (Baars 1993). He believes the human mind has many different specialized systems, which generally exist subconsciously and do not need to communicate with each other. This provides theoretical space for the "integration" of specialists with different representations. According to Baars, consciousness is a kind of "global workspace" that provides a channel for information exchange between different specialized systems. Being more flexible than the AGI model of LIDA built with GWT (global workspace theory) as a template (Baars and Franklin 2009), the foci proposition is a similar global workspace that directly coordinates the specialists on the foci events.

In general terms, global workspace is more like a conference room. Different specialists send and receive information to determine to which part their "attention" should be paid in the proposition. For example, (Cassimatis 2001) there is a system that first recognizes Joe and then Red. What needs to be determined is whether they are the same person. Suppose the system has three specialists performing tasks: a physical location recognition system (a), a color recognition system (b), and a sounding system (c). At this point, (a) and (b) will contradict each other. According to (b), it can be concluded that Red moves from the opposite bank of the river to Joe across the middle but finds that the color of Red (covered in mud) differs from that of Joe. At this time, the higher-level cognition of the system is in need of judging whether they are the same person, in line with the information given by (a), (b), and (c). By this time, (c) is a core system, and the information it gives helps determine that they are an identical person. However, assuming that the colors on Red and Joe are the same, (c) will ask (a) and (b) to review, and even ask (a) to expand the search to the entire map to see if someone has replaced Joe across the bridge. In this case, (b) becomes a core system again. This is simply an example of visual reasoning, and it will involve the highly complex coordination problem of all attribute processors in the framework of mindreading. In reality, different "worlds" mean collaborative contracts for different dedicated systems, and various contracts signify disparate cognitive conditions. To deal with non-coordination, there is a reflective specialist system specifically used to find inconsistencies between the worlds and the resolution of these inconsistencies, thereby forming a "meta consensus" (Cassimatis 2001). It can be seen from the mindreading application that the inheritance function of the external psychological distance can be used as one of the criteria for planning the meta-consensus.

According to the operating mechanism of meta-consensus, Polyscheme seems to be able to monitor external meta-consensus parameters, but it is indeed difficult to complete. The first reason is that Polyscheme's supervision method rests upon frequency supervision to complete the supervision of inherited function reliability. This makes it probable to detect the system's success in obtaining the expected feedback based on the consensus, but the fitting of the inheritance function (assuming that an object is a real person) is a highly statistical result that is based on the actual situation. The convergence of the function is reliable under the same environment, and thus it may be hard to find inconsistencies. The second reason is that under the premise of subject interaction, supervision is sometimes realized through interpersonal interaction and feedback.

Nevertheless, the interaction itself may change the mind of the object, thus breaking the intersubjectivity that has been established before. We can call this interference "*interactive interference*". Moreover, ordinary people do not rely entirely on external parameters to guide their cognition. In fact, humans often cannot directly acquire intersubjective parameters that require complex algorithms to be obtained from the outside world. Instead, some internal overall cognitive experience is often employed to judge the relationship between subjects. We can call this the structure of the subject's cross-temporal identity, or some kind of "personality" or "character", which will be accompanied by the subject's unique way of interacting with the outside world and its judgment criteria. Sometimes human beings judge other people's behavior and inner thoughts through "subjective" methods; this subjectivity is not random but condenses cognitive history development. In other words, the judgment mechanism of meta-consensus should not just originate from the outside world.

However, the formation of meta-consensus is compatible with Bello's computational account of mindreading. The mindreading representation is ascribed to the third-person stimulation, which seems to not match the requirement of the *second-person concept cycle-distributed network*. The third-person stimulation means treating the cost of the inherited function as an objective criterion for the counterfactual inference of mindreading, so the system can "introspect" about the other minds to an exact degree. Nevertheless, mindreading is not necessarily a third-person cognitive process, and so is the self-knowledge about future or past. There is no such universal knowledge unless we presuppose it. And we cannot accept it based on the argument in Sect. 2.

Due to the principle of the knowledge representation and control of Polyscheme, it may have two drawbacks. Its first flaw is to build the self with the event rather than with "history", which means that the self is fragmented and the continuity between egos cannot be guaranteed. A "self" that is not lost in the experience should have a unified representation system and an internal operation mechanism. The experience content displayed by this mechanism can change with the variation of external input experience, but the core mechanics will be invariable. In a sense, this may be some kind of "transcendent" self. According to Piaget's theory (Piaget and Cook 1952), the process of children's mental growth is gradually completed by combining specific perceptions and behaviors with the reflective operation of the original self-mind. Thus, merely a continuous self can guarantee the continuity of moral judgment.

Another drawback of Polyscheme is that its *set of basic possible-world semantics* cannot describe all the distinction and closeness of all possible worlds. And the missing ones may mean those implied by some realistic psychological distance. Here, we introduce David Lewis's possible-world theory to illustrate how the missing ones regularize. According to Lewis's theory, qualitative similarity is more vital than quantitative similarity in theory. Lewis has an analysis of counterfactual dependency causality: "If A, then C". is true if and only if the world in which A and C are both true is more similar to our real world than the one in which A is true but C is false (Lewis 1979, 465). We can write the world in which A and C are both true formally as "W(A&C)", the world in which A is true but C is false as "W(A&¬C)", and the real world as "W(¬A&¬C)". Then, we have $W(A\&C) <_{R(¬A\&¬C)} W(A\&¬C)$, which can be transformed into $W(A\&¬C) <_{R(¬A\&C)} W(A\&C)$. From a quantitative perspective, W(A&C) is farther from the real-world R(¬A&¬C) compared with W(A&¬C), but closer to it in a qualitative sense. Let's use an example of a topology diagram to explain the meaning here (see Figs. 6, 7 and 8). Although Fig. 8 resembles Fig. 7 more than Fig. 9 from a quantitative perspective, Fig. 9 is more similar to Fig.7 in comparison with Fig. 8 from a qualitative angle. Thus, we have Fig. 9 < Fig. 7 Fig. 8.

Fig. 6. Original topology diagram   **Fig. 7.** Topology quantitatively similar to Fig. 6   **Fig. 8.** Topology quantitatively similar to Fig. 6

World similarity in Polyscheme is built on the basis of sets. And in the knowledge representation of mindreading, similarity is constructed on the scale of psychological distance (causal chain length). Suppose that the *increasing* of psychological distance (the lengthening of the cause chain) is set to A, and the *recognition* of some abstract agent causation is set to C (there is no trend change in "real-world" R. For the convenience of processing, we define the decline of the trend as disapproval and the increase as approval). The experimental elements and final results in Knobe and Nichols's paper (2011) are as follows (Table 1):

In the relationship between two items of selective attribution ((1) → (2)), there is A&¬C. Besides, the relationship between the two items of emotional attribution ((3) → (4)) is A&C. We set the former as Wc or W(A&¬C) and the latter as We or W (A&C). Suppose that the *basic* first-person mental state is R, and the variation of the psychological distance in R is zero. According to the knowledge frame of mindreading, if the self is added to the reasoning, there will be C. Therefore, we tend to think that there is ¬A&C in R. Based on Lewis's theory, as long as $W(A\&¬C) <_{R(¬A\&C)} W(A\&C)$ is true,

The Second-Person Standpoint and Moral Machine   131

Table 1. The data of Knobe and Nichols's research about the psychological distance of self

	Background (assuming you observe the following scenario)	Questions (scores 1–7)	Average scores of answers
Choice-Cause (Zoomed-In) (1)	A bee landed next to John, whose hand is drawn back. You know John pulled back because he was afraid of bees	John caused his hand to withdraw	6.10
Choice-Cause (Zoomed-Out) (2)	A bee landed next to John, whose hand was drawn back, and a bottle of milk was knocked over. You know John pulled back because he was afraid of bees	John caused the milk to spill	4.95
Emotion-Caus (Zoomed-In) (3)	A bee landed next to John, with his hand shaking. You know John's hand shakes because he's afraid of bees	John caused his hands to shake	3.95
Emotion-Cause (Zoomed-Out) (4)	A bee landed next to John, with his hands shaking, and a bottle of milk was knocked over. You know John's hands shake because he's afraid of bees	John caused the milk to spill	5.48

we find a counterexample of the mindreading representation concerning Polyscheme. The question now is: Is Wc more similar to R than We? We are inclined to think so.

First, according to (1) → (2), we can see that the lengthening of the causal chain does not necessarily mean the change in psychological distance predicted by C, which shows that the world mechanisms of Wc and We may be different. Second, in terms of selecting attribution, people tend to choose "abstract attribution" from the beginning when there is extremely close psychological distance, which is very close to the state of complete rationalization in R. Even if the cause-effect chain grows, we believe that people will still be apt to perform causal attribution on the target object, and the average answer declines not because people have changed the subject attribution method. Instead, they have joined the investigation of the contingency, and the subject's choice obviously does not cover the milk splash at the far end, which may be defined by people as an accident. This attribution mechanism is clearly more similar to that in the R world. Therefore, we believe that Bello and Bringsjord have simplified the similarity problem in the possible world, and the mindreading representation system has overlooked some experimental results and the significance of Knobe and Nichols's original analysis.

6 Self and Mindreading

If the process of internal consultation in Polyscheme's systems is compared to a meeting, it means that the power to finalize the decision comes from a person in a high position, although his/her decision-making reference comes from some external force. From this point of view, the control of reflective specialists is too strong. Even if the external parameters are relatively objective, the framework setting of the internal possible worlds also results in the situation that parameters are not conducive to establishing a comparatively complete mindreading representation. In addition, it is impossible to establish a complete representation of mindreading knowledge in a sense—at least the *interactive interference* mentioned above may be difficult to avoid. Some people may think that we can try to build a complete system of possible worlds, and then use it as a basis to fit a complete mindreading function. However, this is also a "top-down" approach, which often encounters various types of frame problems in line with judgments by Wendel Wallach et al. (2010).

The core of the problem may not be to establish a complete mindreading frame but to establish a representation that can give timely feedback and adjust the model. Moreover, this is related to the self-knowledge representation of the AGI system and the system's setup ideas as well. A way of avoiding Polycheme's problems can consist of the following: (1) Establish a unified inherent kernel; (2) set up an adaptation mechanism concerning the environment. This requires the system to have an internal control subsystem that can characterize the tendencies within the system and vary as the internal experience changes. Apart from that, the system does not need to pursue too much consistency of internal knowledge, like Polyscheme (although the mechanism of knowledge representation is unified, see Fig. 9), and thus it is not essential to always give a "self" with coordinated functions. The internal control subsystem and external feedback can determine a "self" state when necessary. In this sense, it fits the vision of Fig. 3. Besides, we can design a mindreading representation, as in Fig. 10.

There are few systems in the AGI field that meet the above requirements, and Wang Pei's NARS (the Non-Axiomatic Reasoning System) is considered a potential candidate (Wang 2006). The system follows a kind of non-public logic to establish inference

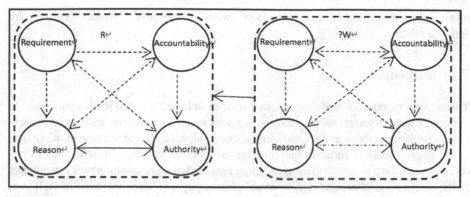

Fig. 9. The dashed boxes represent system boundaries, and the dashed boxes represent different sub-world boundaries

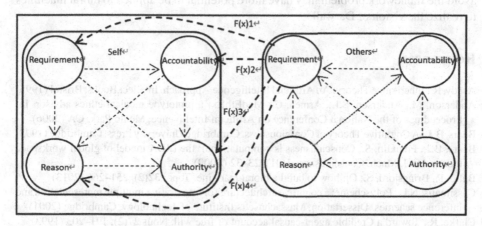

Fig. 10. Architecture inspired by NARS

rules, and its characterization of "propositions" is accomplished through the inheritance relationship between terms. The core of NARS is not a multi-tasking event processor composed of specialists, but a belief network made up of many concepts, whose connotations and extensions are continually changing. NARS follows experience-grounded semantics (EGS), the basic premise of which is *"relatively insufficient knowledge and system resources"* (AIKR) that prevent NARS systems from encountering framework problems. The choice of experience will be based on the system's preference settings— motivation and emotion. It can also determine the representation of self-knowledge, and then the representation of mindreading. Thanks to AIKR, NARS does not need to maintain a constant consistency internally. With the input of external experience, the concept network will change, and unsuitable beliefs will be deleted in principle. Therefore, the relationship between beliefs does not need to be an intact inheritance relationship. Whether it is external information or internal information, it can affect the target concept or belief through intension or extension in the net on the whole. Thus, there may be no need to presuppose the semantic structure of the possible world in NARS to deal with mindreading problems, because there is no explicit conceptual boundary between the self and others.

7 Conclusions

Through our elaboration and analysis, we can draw at least the following conclusions: (1) Darwall's second-person moral philosophy leaves much space for the distributed expression of intersubjectivity and second-person knowledge. (2) Using a single mindreading technique or theory to formulate an inheritance function and using it as an "objective" reference standard to establish a mindreading knowledge representation may run counter to the assumption of second-person moral philosophy. (3) Since this type of AGI system concerning Polyscheme will face various issues in achieving the ideal mindreading representation, an AGI system with unified internal knowledge representation that can avoid the framework problem may have more potential to be applied to moral machines to realize the vision of Darwall.

References

Asady, R.: Inheritance Theory: An Artificial Intelligence Approach. Intellect Books, Bristol (1995)

Anderson, M., Anderson, S.L., Armen, C.: MedEthEx: a prototype medical ethics advisor. In: Proceedings of the National Conference on Artificial Intelligence, Menlo Park, CA (2006)

Baars, B.J.: A Cognitive Theory of Consciousness. Cambridge University Press, Cambridge (1993)

Baars, B.J., Franklin, S.: Consciousness is computational: the LIDA model of global workspace theory. Int. J. Mach. Consciousness 1(01), 23–32 (2009)

Bello, P., Bringsjord, S.: On how to build a moral machine. Topoi 32(2), 251–266 (2013)

Cassimatis, N.L.: Polyscheme: a cognitive architecture for intergrating multiple representation and inference schemes. Dissertation, Massachusetts Institute of Technology, Cambridge (2001)

Clarke, R.: Toward a Credible agent-causal account of free will. Noûs 27(2), 191–203 (1993)

Dameski, A.: A comprehensive ethical framework for AI entities: foundations. Paper Presented at the International Conference on Artificial General Intelligence, Prague, Czech Republic, 22–25 August 2018

Darwall, S.L.: The Second-Person Standpoint: Morality, Respect, and Accountability. Harvard University Press, Cambridge (2006)

Davidson, D.: Essays on Actions and Events: Philosophical Essays Volume 1: Philosophical Essays. Oxford University Press on Demand, Oxford (2001)

Feit, N.: Belief About the Self: A Defense of the Property Theory of Content. Oxford University Press, Oxford (2008)

Gilligan, C.: In a Different Voice: Psychological Theory and Women's Development. Harvard University Press, Cambridge (1993)

Guarini, M.: Computational neural modeling and the philosophy of ethics reflections on the particularism-generalism debate. In: Anderson, M., Anderson, S. (eds.) Machine Ethics, pp. 316–334. Cambridge University Press, Cambridge (2011)

Kim, J.: Causation, nomic subsumption, and the concept of event. J. Philos. 70(8), 217–236 (1973)

Knobe, J., Nichols, S.: Free will and the bounds of the self. In: Kane, R. (ed.) The Oxford Handbook of the Free Will, 2nd edn. (2011). https://philarchive.org/archive/KNOFWA

Lewis, D.: Counterfactual dependence and time's arrow. Noûs 13(4), 455–476 (1979)

McLaren, B.M., Ashley, K.D.: Case-based comparative evaluation in TRUTH-TELLER. In: Proceedings From the Seventeenth Annual Conference of the Cognitive Science Society, Pittburgh, PA (1995)

O'Connor, T.: Why agent causation? Philos. Top. **24**(2), 143–158 (1996)

Piaget, J., Cook, M.T.: The Origins of Intelligence in Children. International Universities Press, New York (1952)

Rawls, J.: Kantian constructivism in moral theory. J. Philos. **77**(9), 515–572 (1980)

Savulescu, J., Maslen, H.: Moral enhancement and artificial intelligence: moral AI? In: Romportl, J., Zackova, E., Kelemen, Jozef (eds.) Beyond artificial intelligence. TIEI, vol. 9, pp. 79–95. Springer, Cham (2015). https://doi.org/10.1007/978-3-319-09668-1_6

Strawson, P.F.: Freedom and Resentment and Other Essays. Routledge, London (2014)

Trope, Y., Liberman, N.: Construal-level theory of psychological distance. Psychol. Rev. **117**(2), 440–463 (2010)

Wallace, R.J.: The Moral Nexus, vol. 9. Princeton University Press, Princeton (2019)

Wallach, W., Allen, C.: Moral Machines: Teaching Robots Right from Wrong. Oxford University Press, Oxford (2008)

Wallach, W., Franklin, S., Allen, C.: A conceptual and computational model of moral decision making in human and artificial agents. Top. Cogn. Sci. **2**(3), 454–485 (2010)

Wang, P.: Rigid Flexibility: The Logic of Intelligence (Applied Logic Series 34). Springer, New York (2006)

Williams, B.: Shame and Necessity, vol. 57. University of California Press, Berkeley (2008)

Author Index

Printed in the United States
by Baker & Taylor Publisher Services

Printed in the United States
by Baker & Taylor Publisher Services